NORTHCOUNTRY
KITCHENS
COOKBOOK

Avery Color Studios, Inc.
Gwinn, Michigan 49841

Published by:
Avery Color Studios, Inc.
Gwinn, Michigan 49841

Copyright 1980 by Avery Color Studios

First Edition—1980
Reprinted—1983, 1985, 1987, 1989,
1990, 1991, 1994, 1996, 1998, 2003

ISBN 0-932212-21-2
Library of Congress Catalog Card No. 94-077921

Illustrations by:
John Evans
Marquette, Michigan

Featuring over 500 recipes, many Finnish and Swedish, contributed by the finest Northcountry cooks.

We wish to express our sincere *Thanks* to members of the Joanna Circle, Sion Lutheran Church, Chatham, Michigan, and the following individuals for the contributions which made *The Northcountry Kitchens Cookbook* possible:

Jane Aho	Marilyn Kallio	Audrey Pokela
Lauri Ahonen	Evelyn Keskimaki	Jill Pokela
Hazel V. Akkala	Harriet Kienitz	Marion Pokela
Anne Balko	Judy Kienitz	Phyllis Pokela
Ray Berg	Nancy Kirby	Ruth Pokela
Elsie Bubnash	Kathy Kolpack	Marion Pulkkinen
Vivian Carlson	Elma Koski	Jean Quaal
Beth Dawson	Lillian Kresovich	Helen M. Rockhill
Carol Erkkila	Leah Lahti	Jennie Rukkila
Louise Fulcher	Rose C. Lemin	Eva Ruska
Alice Goin	Mildred Lindfors	Margaret St. Onge
Viena Harju	Sadie Lindholm	Midge Salminen
Madge Hollander	Joanne Linn	Helen Salo
Mabel Hollender	Pam McCollum	Ina Samuelson
Ethel Holmquist	Ada Maki	Debbie Sandstrom
Carol Hurston	Hella Maki	Verna Schmidt
Ellen Hyry	Ruth Maki	Norma Scovill
Patty Hyry	O. Makinen	Gertrude Sequin
Hilia Ihamaki	Ellen Nelson	Thelma Sippolu
Olive Ekkala	Helen Norman	Judy Socha
Beatrice Johnson	Pat Nybeck	Dorothy Swajanen
Irene Johnson	Irene Obenauf	Anja Vincent
Peggy Johnson	Tynne Oja	Aili Ylitalo
Bernice Kallio	Dorothy Paul	Senia Ylinen
Joy Kallio	Mary Piippo	

Weights and Measures
Standard Abbreviations

t.	teaspoon	pt.	pint	oz.	ounce
T.	tablespoon	qt.	quart	lb.	pound
c.	cup	d.b.	double boiler	pk.	peck
f.g.	few grains	B.P.	baking powder	bu.	bushel

Guide to Weights and Measures

1 teaspoon=60 drops
3 teaspoons=1 tablespoon
2 tablespoons=1 fluid ounce
4 tablespoons=1/4 cup
5-1/3 tablespoons=1/3 cup
8 tablespoons=1/2 cup
16 tablespoons=1 cup

1 pound=16 ounces
1 cup=1/2 pint
2 cups=1 pint
4 cups=1 quart
4 quarts=1 gallon
8 quarts=1 peck
4 pecks=1 bushel

Substitutions and Equivalents

2 tablespoons of fat=1 ounce
1 cup of fat=1/2 pound
1 pound of butter=2 cups
1 cup of hydrogenated fat plus
   1/2 t. salt=1 cup butter
2 cups sugar=1 pound
2-1/2 cups packed brown sugar=
   1 pound
1-1/3 cups packed brown sugar=
   1 cup of granulated sugar
3-1/2 cups of powdered sugar=
   1 pound
4 cups sifted all purpose flour=1 pound
4-1/2 cups sifted cake flour=1 pound
1 ounce bitter chocolate=1 square

4 tablespoons cocoa plus 2 teaspoons butter=
   1 ounce of bitter chocolate
1 cup egg whites=8 to 10 whites
1 cup egg yolks=12 or 14 yolks
16 marshmallows=1/4 pound
1 tablespoon cornstarch=2 tablespoons flour
   for thickening
1 tablespoon vinegar or lemon juice & 1 cup
   milk=1 cup sour milk
10 graham crackers=1 cup fine crumbs
1 cup whipping cream=2 cups whipped
1 cup evaporated milk=3 cups whipped
1 lemon=3 to 4 tablespoons juice
1 orange=6 to 8 tablespoons juice
1 cup uncooked rice=3 to 4 cups cooked rice

Table of Contents

Approximate Amounts to Serve 50 People

Navy beans for baking ....3 qts. or 6 lbs.

Canned string beans ....2 No. 10 cans

Canned beets...2 No. 10 cans

Roast beef ....20 lbs.

Roast beef for Swiss steak—3/4 inch thick ....20 lbs.

Ground meat for loaf ....10 lbs.

Butter...1-1/2 lbs.

Chicken (roasted) ....30 lbs.

Chicken pie..20 lbs.

Coffee ....1 lb.

Baked ham...2 hams 10 to 12 lbs. each

Ice cream—dessert ....2 gal.

Ice cream—for pie ....1 gal.

Lettuce...1 oz. per salad

Head lettuce salad...7 lbs.

Salted nuts...1-1/2 lbs.

Olives ....2 qts.

Oysters (escalloped)..1 gal.

Peas..2 No. 10 cans

Peas and carrots...1 No. 10 can and 5 lbs. carrots

Roast pork or fresh ham..20 lbs.

Pork chops...18 lbs.

Potatoes (mashed)...1-1/4 pecks

Sweet potatoes...13-1/2 lbs.

Rice...3 lbs.

Rolls...100 rolls

Soup ....3 gal.

Turkey ....22-25 lbs.

Vegetables (fresh—beans, beets, carrots or cabbage) ....10 lbs.

Whipped cream ....2 pts.

Approximate 100 Calorie Portions

Almonds (shelled)—12-15
Angel cake—1-3/4 inch
    cube
Apple—1 large
Apple pie—1/3 normal
    piece
Apricots—5 large
Asparagus—20 large
    stalks
Bacon—4 to 5 small slices
Bananas—1 medium
Baked Beans—1/3 c.
    canned
Beans, green string—
    2-1/2 c.
Beets—1-1/3 c. sliced
Bread—all kinds—slice
    1/2 inch thick
Butter—1 T.
Buttermilk—1-1/8 c.
Cabbage—4 to 5 c.
    shredded
Cake—1-3/4 inch cube
Candy—1 inch cube
Cantaloupe—1 medium
Carrots—1-2/3 c.
Cauliflower—1 small
    head
Celery—4 c.
Cereal—uncooked—
    3/4 c.
Cheese—1-1/8 inch cube
Cottage cheese—5 T.
Cherries, sweet, fresh—20
Cookies—1, up to 3"
    diam.
Corn—1/3 c.

Crackers—4 soda or
    2-1/2 graham
Cream, thick—1 T.
Cream, thin—4 T.
Cream sauce—4 T.
Dates—3 to 4
Doughnuts—1/2
Eggs—1-1/3 egg
Fish, fat—size of 1 chop
Fish, lean—size of 2 chops
Flour—4 T.
Frankfurter—1 small
French dressing—1-1/2 T.
Grapefruit—1/2 large
Grape juice—1/2 c.
Grapes—20
Gravy—2 T.
Ice cream—1/4 c.
Lard—1 T.
Lemons—3 large
Lettuce—2 large heads
Macaroni—3/4 c. cooked
Malted milk—3 T.
Marmalade/jelly—1 T.
Marshmallows—5
Mayonnaise—1 T.
Meat, cold, sliced—1/8"
    slice
Meat, fat—size 1/2 chop
Meat, lean—size 1 chop
Milk, regular—5/8 c.
Molasses—1-1/2 T.
Onions—3 to 4 medium
Oranges—1 large
Orange juice—1 c.
Peaches, fresh—3 medium
Peanut butter—1 T.

Pears, fresh—2 medium
Peas, canned—3/4 c.
Peacans—12 meats
Pie—1/4 ordinary serving
Pineapple—2 slices 1"
    thick
Plums—3 to 4 large
Popcorn—1-1/2 c.
Potatoes, sweet—1/2
    medium
Potatoes, white—
    1 medium
Potato salad—1 c.
Prunes, dried—4
Radishes—3 dozen
Raisins—1/4 c.
Rhubarb, stewed and
    sweetened—1/2 c.
Rice, cooked—3/4 c.
Rolls—1 medium
Rutabagas—1-2/3 c.
Sausage—2 small
Sauerkraut—2-1/2 c.
Sherbet—4 T.
Spinach—2-1/2 c.
Squash—1 c.
Strawberries—1-1/3 c.
Sugar, brown—3 T.
Sugar, white—2 T.
Tomatoes, canned—2 c.
Tomatoes, fresh—2 to 3
    medium
Turnips—2 c.
Walnuts—8 to 16 meats
Watermelon—3/4" slice

Mealtime Prayers

Come, Lord Jesus, be our Guest:
And let these gifts to us be blest.
May our souls by Thee be fed
Ever on the Living Bread.

Amen

Father, bless the food we take,
And bless us all for Jesus' sake.

Amen

For food and all Thy gifts of love,
We give Thee thanks and praise
Look down, O Jesus, from above,
And bless us all our days.

Amen

Give us this day our daily bread.

Matthew 6:11

God bless not only food and drink
But what we do and what we think
And grant for all our work and play,
That we may love Thee more each day.

In Jesus' Name, Amen

Oh give thanks unto the Lord;
for He is good . . .
Who Giveth food to all flesh,
for His mercy endureth forever.

Psalm 136

Breads, Sweet Rolls, Pancakes and Doughnuts

Applesauce Nut Honey Bread

1/3 c. light molasses
1/3 c. honey
1/3 c. water
1 c. sweetened applesauce
2-1/4 c. flour
1/2 c. bran

1 t. salt
1 t. soda
1/2 t. baking powder
2 eggs
1/2 c. nuts mixed with 1 T. flour

Mix ingredients in order given, beating thoroughly. Bake in foil lined loaf pan at 350° for 55 minutes. Remove from pan while warm. Cool on rack.

Pumpkin Quick Bread

2/3 c. shortening
2-2/3 c. sugar
4 eggs
1 can (1 lb.) pumpkin
2/3 c. water
3-1/2 c. flour
2 t. soda

1-1/2 t. salt
1/2 t. baking powder
1 t. cinnamon
1 t. cloves
2/3 c. nuts (chopped)
2/3 c. raisins

Heat oven to 350°. Grease 2 loaf pans or 1 tube angel food pan.

Cream shortening and sugar thoroughly. Add eggs, pumpkin, and water. Blend in dry ingredients, except nuts and raisins. Stir in nuts and raisins. Bake in prepared pans 65 to 75 minutes, until a wooden pick inserted in center comes out clean.

Shaker Brown Bread

1 c. rye flour
1 c. corn meal
1 c. graham flour
1 t. salt
3/4 t. soda

1-3/4 c. sour milk
3/4 c. molasses
2 T. butter (melted)
1 c. raisins (chopped; optional)

Sift dry ingredients and mix well. Combine in large bowl the sour milk, molasses and melted butter. Combine the 2 mixtures and stir thoroughly, adding lightly floured raisins. Pour into 2 buttered molds, fill only 2/3 full. Steam for 2 hours and then bake for 1/2 hour.

Gumdrop Nut Bread

3 c. Bisquick
1/2 c. sugar
1 egg

1-1/4 c. milk
1/2 c. nuts (chopped)
1 c. small gumdrops (cut up)

Heat oven to 350°; grease loaf pan, 9 x 5 x 3 inches. Mix Bisquick, sugar, egg, and milk. Beat vigorously with spoon 1/2 minute. Stir in nuts and gumdrops. Pour into pan. Bake at 350° for 50-55 minutes. Cool before removing from pan and slicing. Slice very thin and spread with cream cheese.

Carrot-Coconut Bread

2 c. flour
2 t. baking soda
2 t. cinnamon
Dash of salt
1-1/2 c. sugar
1/2 c. chopped nuts
1/2 c. crushed pineapple, drained

1 c. oil
3 eggs
2 t. vanilla
2 c. grated carrots
1 c. raisins
1/2 c. coconut

Bake at 325° for 1 hour in a greased and floured 10" tube pan.

There is no spectacle on earth more appealing than that of a beautiful woman in the act of cooking dinner for someone she loves.

Thomas Wolfe

Spiced Raisin Muffins

2 c. prepared biscuit mix
1/4 c. sugar
1/2 t. ground cinnamon

1 c. raisins (finely cut)
1 egg (slightly beaten)
3/4 c. milk

Combine biscuit mix, sugar, cinnamon and raisins. Blend together egg and milk; add to dry ingredients. Stir until batter is just moistened. Bake in hot oven 425° about 15 minutes. Makes 12 muffins.

Lemon Bread

1/2 c. shortening
1 c. sugar
1 lemon rind (grated)
2 eggs

1/2 c. milk
1-1/2 c. flour
1 t. baking powder
1/4 t. salt

Juice of lemon

1/4 c. powdered sugar

Mix as per usual first 8 ingredients. Bake in a bread pan 50 to 60 minutes at 350°. Remove loaf from pan while still hot and drizzle with a sauce made of lemon juice and powdered sugar. Freezes well.

Sour Cream Coffee Cake

SIFT TOGETHER:
2 c. flour (sifted)
1/2 t. soda

1 t. baking powder
1/4 t. salt

CREAM TOGETHER:
1 c. margarine
2 eggs
1 t. vanilla

1-1/4 c. sugar
1 c. sour cream

MIX TOGETHER:
1/2 c. nuts
1 t. cinnamon

3 T. sugar

Cream together margarine and sugar, add eggs and mix thoroughly. Add alternately sour cream, dry ingredients and vanilla. Grease and flour pan. Add half the batter to pan. Sprinkle with 3/4 of the nut, sugar, and cinnamon mixture. Add remaining batter, then sprinkle remaining nut mixture on top. Bake 350° for 1 hour.

Banana Bread

1/2 c. shortening
1 c. sugar
2 eggs
1 t. vanilla
3 medium bananas (mashed)

1 t. soda
1 t. salt
2 c. flour
nuts (as much as desired)

Cream sugar and shortening together. Beat eggs, then add eggs and vanilla to sugar and shortening. Sift dry ingredients together. Add with bananas to sugar and shortening and eggs. Fold in chopped nuts. Bake in greased loaf pan for 1 hour at 350°.

Banana Bread

1/2 c. butter or oleo
1 c. sugar
3 eggs (slightly beaten)
3 ripe bananas (crush with fork)
1-1/4 T. sour milk
1 T. lemon juice

2 c. flour
1/2 t. salt
1/2 t. soda
1-1/2 t. baking powder
1 c. nut meats
1/2 c. dates

Cream butter and sugar; add remaining ingredients in order given. Bake at 350° for 45 minutes.

Banana Cherry Bread

1/2 c. shortening
1 c. sugar
2 eggs
1/2 c. nuts (chopped)

3 bananas (mashed)
2 c. flour
1 t. soda
1 bottle maraschino cherries (do not cut)

Cream shortening and sugar, beat in eggs. Add mashed bananas, then flour and soda. Carefully stir in cherries (left whole) and nuts. Makes 2 loaves, but if recipe is doubled it will make 3 generous loaves. Bake at 350° for 45 to 50 minutes.

A kitchen is a friendly place
Full of living's daily grace
And rich in dignity is she
Who shares in its hospitality

Fresh Carrot Bread

2/3 c. butter	1 t. cinnamon
1 c. sugar	1/4 t. salt
2 large eggs	1 c. carrots (finely grated)
1-1/2 c. flour	1 c. seedless raisins
2 t. baking powder	1/2 c. nuts (chopped)

Place butter in mixing bowl; gradually blend in sugar, beat in eggs. Sift together flour, baking powder, cinnamon, and salt. Gradually add to mixture. Mix carrots, raisins, and nuts; stir into batter. Turn into well greased, lightly floured 9 x 5 x 3 inch loaf pan.

Bake in preheated moderate oven 350° for about 1 hour. Cool in pan 10 minutes; turn onto wire rack to finish cooling. Keep bread 1 day before serving. Serve with butter or cream cheese.

To store wrap tightly in aluminum foil. Makes 1 loaf.

Lemon Spice Puffs

1 pkg. dry yeast	2 eggs (beaten)
1/4 c. water	1 T. lemon rind (grated)
3/4 c. milk (scalded)	1 t. lemon juice
1/3 c. shortening	3 c. all-purpose flour
6 T. sugar	3 T. sugar
1 t. salt	1 t. cinnamon

Soften yeast in lukewarm water. Combine milk, shortening, sugar and salt in mixing bowl. Stir to combine. Cool to lukewarm and add eggs, lemon rind, lemon juice and yeast mixture. Mix well.

Gradually add the flour, beating well after each addition. Cover and let rise in warm place, until light and double in size, about 1 to 1-1/2 hours. Drop by spoonfuls into well greased muffin pans, filling about half full.

Combine sugar and cinnamon; sprinkle over batter in pans. Cover and let rise in warm place until light and doubled in size, about 30 minutes. Bake in 375° oven 15-20 minutes. Makes 1-1/2 to 2 dozen.

Finnish Christmas Bread *(Joulu Limppu)*

1-1/2 qt. warm water
10 large potatoes
3 c. rye flour
3/4 c. molasses
1-1/2 c. brown sugar
1 t. anise seed
1 t. caraway seed

1 T. salt
1 cake fresh yeast
1/4 lb. oleo (margarine)
1/4 lb. lard
white flour
Topping (recipe follows)

Cook and mash potatoes. Mix with warm water and rye flour and let set overnight.

Dissolve yeast with small amount of warm water and add to rye flour and potato mixture. Add remaining ingredients. Knead in enough white flour so dough doesn't stick to hands. Let rise. Shape into loaves. Bake at 400° for about 20 minutes. Then at 300° for 45 minutes. Yields 5 loaves.

TOPPING

While still warm spread with a mixture of melted butter, water, brown sugar and dark syrup which has been boiled. Runny mixture.

Oatmeal Bread

1-1/4 c. boiling water
1 c. quick cooking oatmeal
1/2 c. molasses
1/3 c. shortening
1 T. salt

2 cakes compressed yeast or
    2 pkg. dried yeast
1/2 c. lukewarm water
2 eggs (beaten)
flour

Mix water, oatmeal, molasses, shortening, and salt. Set aside to cool to lukewarm.

Dissolve yeast in 1/2 c. lukewarm water. Add 2 c. flour to molasses mixture and beat well. Add yeast and eggs, beat well. Add enough flour to make a soft dough. Turn onto lightly floured board. Cover and let rest 10 minutes. Knead until smooth. Place in greased bowl and let rise 1-1/2 hours or until double in bulk.

Shape into 2 loaves. Grease bread pans, sprinkle each pan with 2 T. rolled oats. Place loaves in pans, cover and let rise until double in bulk. Bake at 375° for 35-40 minutes. Brush tops with butter. Cool on a rack.

Blueberry Freezer Bread

3 c. unsifted flour
2 t. baking powder
1 t. baking soda
1/2 t. salt
1-1/2 t. lemon juice
1 c. chopped nuts
2/3 c. shortening

1-1/2 c. sugar
4 eggs
1/2 c. milk
1 c. crushed pineapple, drained
1/2 c. flaked coconut
2 c. fresh blueberries

Sift flour, baking powder, soda and salt. Cream shortening until light and fluffy. Beat in sugar. Stir in eggs, milk, lemon juice and pineapple. Beat in dry ingredients. Fold in blueberries, nuts and coconut. Pour dough into 2 greased and floured bread pans. Bake at 350° for 45 minutes.

Rye Bread *(Very Old Recipe)*

1 qt. warm water
2 pkg. yeast dissolved in 1/2 c. warm water

2-1/2 to 3 c. rye flour

3 t. salt

8 c. or more white flour

Mix first 3 ingredients the night before and put to rise in warm place.

Second step: In morning, cut down and add salt and flour, adding flour gradually at first, then knead dough for 10 minutes. Rise in warm place until double in bulk. Cut down and knead a little and put into pans. Makes about 4 loaves. Bake 40-50 minutes at 400°.

Vegetable Bread

1 c. oil
1 c. sugar
3 eggs, separated
3 t. hot water
1 c. grated carrots
1 c. grated raw beets

2 c. flour
2 t. baking powder
1/4 t. salt
1 t. cinnamon
1 t. vanilla

Beat together egg yolks, oil, sugar, water and vanilla. Stir in carrots and beets. Blend in the dry ingredients. Beat egg whites until stiff and fold in. Bake in a greased and floured 10" tube pan or in 2 loaf pans at 350° for 45 minutes.

Vienna Bread

2-1/2 c. warm water (not hot)	1 pkg. Fleischmann's dry yeast
1 T. sugar	8 c. flour (sifted)
1 T. salt	2 T. shortening (soft)

Measure water, sugar, and salt into large mixing bowl. Add yeast and stir to dissolve. Add 2 c. flour, beat until blended. Stir in 2 T. soft shortening and remaining flour. Mix in with hands. Turn out on board and knead until smooth and elastic. Put in greased bowl. Cover with towel and let rise until double in bulk. Divide in 2 parts, form into balls and cover on board. Let rest 15 minutes. Shape into 2 long tapered loaves and place on baking sheet sprinkled with cornmeal. Cover and let rise in warm place, free from draft, until double. Brush with cornstarch glaze. Make 4 diagonal gashes on top of loaves and sprinkle with poppy seeds. Bake at 450° for 10 minutes. Then lower heat to 350° and bake until done about 30-40 minutes longer.

VERY IMPORTANT: Place a large pan of hot water on lower shelf and bread on upper shelf. Keep water in during baking or crust will dry out.

CORNSTARCH GLAZE

1/2 c. cold water	1/2 t. salt
1 t. cornstarch	

Combine ingredients in saucepan. Cook over medium heat, stirring constantly until mixture thickens.

Coffee Cake

3 egg yolks	3 T. sugar
1/2 c. milk	1 t. vanilla
1/2 lb. butter	1 dry yeast in 1/2 c. lukewarm water
3 c. flour	

Scald milk and add butter. Cool to lukewarm. Beat egg yolks and sugar, add milk and yeast to egg mixture; alternate with flour, working dough until it leaves spoon. Put dough in refrigerator overnight. Divide dough and roll thin, melt a little butter and brush on top and sides.

FILLING

Beat 3 egg whites stiff, fold in 2/3 c. sugar and 1 c. nuts. Roll as jelly roll. Makes 3 coffee cakes. Bake at 350° for 35 to 45 minutes.

Swedish Hardtack

1/2 t. soda	1/3 c. brown sugar
1 c. buttermilk	6 T. shortening
3 c. white flour	1 t. baking powder
1 c. whole wheat flour	1-1/2 t. salt

Mix soda in milk. Mix dry ingredients; then work in brown sugar and shortening as for pie crust. Add milk and soda. Roll very thin. Place on cookie sheets and bake at 425° until brown.

German Stollen

1 pkg. dry yeast	2-3/4 c. flour (sifted; about)
1/4 c. lukewarm water	1 egg (beaten)
3/4 c. milk	1/4 c. raisins
2 T. shortening	1/2 c. mixed fruit (candied)
1/4 c. sugar	2 T. butter (melted)
1-1/2 t. salt	powdered sugar icing
1 t. lemon rind (grated; optional)	1/3 c. nuts (chopped)

Sprinkle yeast into water, let stand 5 minutes, stir smooth. Scald milk, add shortening, sugar, salt, and lemon rind. Cool to lukewarm. Sift flour, measure. Add yeast to milk; add egg; add 1 cup flour, beat thoroughly. Add raisins and fruit, add enough flour to make a soft dough, turn out on lightly floured board; knead in remaining flour. When smooth, place in greased bowl. Cover, let rise in warm place until doubled in size. Turn dough out on board, roll into an oval 3/4 inch thick. Brush 1/2 of oval with melted butter, fold over like large Parker House roll (or divide dough and make 2 smaller versions.) Do not press edges together. Place on greased baking sheet, let rise double again. Bake in moderate oven, 350°, about 30 minutes. Spread lightly with icing, sprinkle with nuts.

Rye Bread

1-1/2 qts. warm water	1/2 c. oleo
3/4 c. sugar	3 c. coarse rye flour
2 T. salt	3 T. molasses
3 pkg. dry yeast	3 T. dark corn syrup

Dissolve yeast in warm water, add oleo, sugar, salt, molasses and syrup. Add rye flour, then add as much white flour as needed. Let rise in bowl, shape into loaves and let rise about 1 hour. Bake at 350° for 45 minutes to 1 hour.

Coffee Cake

5 c. flour	2 cakes yeast in 1/4 c. lukewarm water
1 t. salt	1 c. warm milk
1/2 c. sugar	3 eggs (beaten)
1 c. shortening	1 t. vanilla

Sift dry ingredients. Cut in shortening as for pie crust. Mix rest of the ingredients. Add all at once. Mix only enough to dampen. Place in refrigerator overnight. Divide in half or thirds. Spread with filling:

FILLING

1 c. sugar or brown sugar	1/4 c. butter or margarine
1 T. cinnamon	Nuts (if desired)

Roll dough as for jelly roll. Spread on filling. Shape in ring or leave straight. Slit top if desired. Let rise 2 hours. Bake at 350° about 30 minutes. Frost if desired. Makes 2 large or 3 small cakes.

Swedish Rye Bread

2 c. medium rye flour	1 T. anise seed (optional)
3/4 c. brown sugar	3 T. soft shortening
2 c. warm water	1 T. molasses
1 dry yeast	white flour
1 T. salt	

Combine everything but white flour to make sponge. Let rise in warm place at least 1 hour. Stir down and add white flour kneading on floured surface to make soft dough. Divide to make 2 loaves. Rise until doubled in loaf pans. Bake 1 hour at 325°. Do not rise fully second time as it will finish process while baking.

Cardamom Coffee Cake

5 crushed cardamom seed in 2 c. milk (scalded)	1 stick oleo (melted in milk)

Cool to lukewarm. Add 2 pkg. dry yeast dissolved in 1/4 c. warm water and 2 beaten eggs; in large bowl 1 c. granulated sugar, 1-1/2 t. salt, and 4 c. flour. Add wet ingredients to dry and knead in enough more flour to make a smooth, not heavy dough. Let rise until double. Form braided loaves and let rise again. Bake at 375° for 30-40 minutes. Brush with coffee, butter, sugar mixture and sprinkle dry sugar on top.

Sticky Buns

3/4 c. milk	3 eggs (beaten)
1/2 c. sugar	4-2/3 c. flour (about; sifted)
1-1/4 t. salt	3/4 c. soft margarine
1/2 c. margarine	2 c. dark brown sugar
1/3 c. warm water	1 c. pecans (coarsely chopped)
2 pkg. dry yeast	3/4 c. maple-blended syrup

Scald milk, stir in sugar, salt and 1/2 c. margarine; cool to lukewarm. Measure warm water into large bowl; sprinkle yeast and dissolve. Add lukewarm milk mixture, eggs and half of flour. Beat well. Stir in remaining flour with spoon to make a soft dough. On a floured board knead until smooth and elastic, about 8 minutes. Place in greased bowl, and grease top. Cover and let rise until double in bulk.

While dough is rising prepare pans. Use 3 deep 9 inch pie plates or 8 x 8 x 2 inch pans. Spread 2 T. of soft margarine in each pan. Sprinkle 1/2 c. brown sugar and 1/3 c. pecans in each pan.

Punch dough down and turn on floured board. Divide into 3 parts. Roll each part into rectangle 9 inches long and 1/2 inch thick. Spread each with some of the remaining soft margarine; sprinkle with remaining brown sugar. Roll each up from long side and cut into 9 slices. Arrange 9 rolls in each pan, cut sides up. Cover, let rise in warm place about 1/2 hour or until double in bulk. Pour 1/2 c. syrup over rolls in each pan. Bake in hot oven, 400°, about 20-25 minutes or until done. Cool in pans 10 minutes, invert into plates to finish cooling. Makes 27 rolls.

Whole Wheat Hard Rolls *(20 Rolls)*

2 c. warm water	1 T. oleo
1 pkg. dry yeast	2-1/2 c. whole wheat flour
1 T. sugar	2-3/4 c. white flour (about)
2 t. salt	1 egg white (unbeaten)

Measure water in bowl, add yeast, sugar, salt, oleo, and wheat flour to make soft dough. Beat till smooth. Add white flour gradually. Knead. Place in greased bowl, grease top. Cover. Let rise about 1 hour. Punch down and form into rolls, about 20. Let rise and bake 425°, 15 to 20 minutes. Brush with egg white and bake 2 minutes more.

Cinnamon Leaves

2 c. milk	1/2 c. butter or oleo
2 cakes yeast	3 eggs (beaten)
1/4 c. lukewarm water	1/2 t. salt
3/4 c. sugar	melted butter and cinnamon-sugar
Approx. 6-1/2 c. flour (sifted)	

Scald milk and cool to lukewarm; add 2 T. sugar. Soften yeast in lukewarm water until it dissolves. Then add eggs, butter, salt, sugar and flour, knead until smooth and velvety. Let rise until double in size.

Roll out dough and cut with round cookie cutter 1/4 inch deep. Dip each piece in melted butter, then in mixture of cinnamon and sugar. Place 1 against the other (circles on edge) in pan. Let rise until double in size. Bake at 350° for 30-35 minutes.

Biscuit *(Sweet Roll Dough)*

1-1/2 qt. warm water	1/4 lb. margarine
10 cardamom seeds (crushed)	1/4 lb. butter
3 eggs	1 cake fresh yeast
1-1/2 c. sugar	flour
1 t. salt	

Mix crushed cardamom seed with warm water. Add all remaining ingredients and enough white flour so dough doesn't stick to hands. Let rise twice in warm place. Roll out 1/3 of dough into oblong. Spread with soft butter, cinnamon and sugar. Roll up and cut into 1 inch slices and place in pan. Repeat with 1/3 dough. With remaining 1/3 dough divide into 3 balls. Roll out into oblong and make braid. Let rise. Bake at 375° for 35 to 40 minutes.

After baking while still warm, spread with a mixture of sugar, butter and water which has been boiled. Sprinkle with sugar.

Potato Pancakes

2 c. potatoes	1/2 t. baking powder
3 T. flour	1/2 c. milk
2 eggs	1 t. salt

Grind potatoes in food chopper, beat the eggs. Add all ingredients together and mix well. Fry on greased griddle; electric fry pan works well. Potato pancakes take longer to fry than others.

Apple Squares

2/3 c. milk (scalded)
  (cool to lukewarm)

1 c. Crisco
2-1/2 c. flour
3 egg yolks (beaten)

1 T. sugar
1 oz. cake yeast or pkg.

canned pie filling
(apple, cherry or peach)

Combine milk, sugar, and yeast. Mix flour and shortening as for pie crust. Add milk mixture and egg yolks. Mix well. Divide into 2 equal parts and roll to fit 12 x 14 inch pan. Pour in pie filling and spread evenly. Place on top dough and seal the edges. Let rise 1 hours. Bake at 350° for 30 minutes. Frost with powdered sugar icing.

Cheese Twists

1-3/4 c. all-purpose flour (sifted)
2-1/2 t. baking powder
3/4 t. salt
1 T. onion (minced)
2/3 c. buttermilk
3 T. butter (melted)

1/2 jar (5 oz. size) bacon-cheese or
  sharp cheese spread
2 T. parsley (minced)
1/4 c. butter (melted)
2 T. Parmesan cheese (grated)

Sift flour with baking powder and salt. Stir in onion. Combine buttermilk with 3 T. melted butter. Stir into dry ingredients, forming a soft dough. Roll into a 12 x 10 inch rectangle. Melt cheese over hot water. Spread cheese over entire length of dough and about 2/3 width. Sprinkle parsley over cheese. Fold plain third of dough over center third; fold remaining third of dough over the 2 layers. Press dough gently with rolling pin. Cut into 1 inch wide strips; dip in 1/4 c. melted butter, coating all sides. Twist each piece twice. Place on buttered cookie sheet; sprinkle with grated cheese. Bake at 400° for about 12 minutes or until delicately brown. Remove from cookie sheet immediately.

Kropsu *(Finnish pancake)*

2 eggs
1/2 c. sugar
1/2 t. salt

3/4 c. flour
3 c. milk
2 t. butter in each pan

Mix all the ingredients together in a large bowl. Butter the pans. Preheat oven to 475°, later reduce to 375° for 20-30 minutes baking time.

Finnish Coffee Bread

1 pkg. dry yeast	2 eggs
2 c. warm milk (scalded and cooled)	1 t. salt
6 c. flour	8 cardamom seeds (crushed)
1 c. sugar	1/2 c. butter (soft)

Dissolve yeast in warm milk. Add sugar, salt, beaten eggs and crushed seeds. Add flour, mixing well with spoon. (You may need to use slightly more flour.) Lastly add soft butter, working in with hands, cover and rise. Roll out into desired shapes and rise again. Bake at 350° for about 25 minutes. May brush with beaten egg white and sprinkle with sugar before baking. Makes 2 coffee breads.

Coffee Cake

1/2 lb. butter	2 eggs
4 c. flour	1 c. milk
1 t. salt	2 fresh yeast
2 T. sugar	

FILLING

1/2 c. nuts	1-1/2 c. sugar
1 t. cinnamon	1/4 lb. butter

Mix flour and butter as for pie crust. Crumble yeast into mixture. Beat eggs and add milk, sugar, salt, and add to flour mixture. Mix well. Refrigerate overnight. Roll 1/2 dough to 1/4 inch thick. Spread filling and roll like a jelly roll. Bake 375° for 25 minutes.

Potato Cheese Waffles

3 eggs—beat until light

ADD:

1 c. milk	1/2 t. salt
2 T. butter (melted)	2 c. potatoes (mashed)
1 c. flour	1/2 c. shredded cheese
2 t. baking powder	

Mix all ingredients well and bake on waffle iron.

Coffee Cake

3/4 c. butter
1 c. sugar
2 eggs (beaten)
1 c. sour cream
2-1/2 c. flour
1 t. salt

1 t. soda
1 can pie filling (1 lb. 5 oz.) cherry, raisin,
   peach, or apple, etc.
1/2 c. sugar
1/2 t. cinnamon

Cream butter and sugar. Combine eggs and sour cream. Add to first mixture. Stir in flour, salt and soda, mix well. Spread half of batter in greased 9 x 13 inch pan. Spread pie filling over batter and combine sugar and cinnamon, sprinkle half over pie filling. Top with remaining batter, sprinkle with remaining sugar and cinnamon. Garnish with nuts. Bake at 350° for 45 minutes.

Potato Doughnuts

3 eggs
2/3 c. sugar
1 c. cold mashed potatoes
2 T. shortening (melted)
1 t. vanilla

3 c. flour
1/2 t. nutmeg
1/4 c. milk
3/4 t. salt
3 t. baking powder

Beat eggs, add sugar and stir in potatoes, shortening, and vanilla. Add dry ingredients alternately with milk. Chill dough and pat out about 1/4 inch thick. Cut and fry. Makes 3-1/2 to 4 dozen.

Blueberry Coffee Cake

3/4 c. sugar
1/4 c. soft shortening
1 egg
1/2 c. milk

2 c. flour
2 t. baking powder
Pinch of salt
2 c. blueberries

Mix sugar, shortening, and egg; stir in milk, flour, baking powder and salt. Fold in blueberries. Put in 9 x 13 inch greased pan.

TOPPING

1 c. sugar
1 t. cinnamon

2/3 c. flour
1/2 c. soft butter

Combine ingredients. Sprinkle on batter. Bake at 350° for 50 minutes.

Honey Graham Bread

2 c. milk
1/3 c. honey
1 t. salt
1/4 c. margarine
1/2 c. warm water

2 cakes yeast or 2 pkg dry yeast
2-1/2 c. graham flour (unsifted)
3-3/4 c. white flour (unsifted;
   approximately)

Scald milk. Add honey, salt, and margarine. Cool to lukewarm. Measure warm water into large warm bowl. Sprinkle or crumble in yeast. Add lukewarm milk mixture, graham flour and 2 c. white flour. Beat until smooth. Stir in enough additional white flour to make a soft dough.

Turn out onto a lightly floured board and knead until smooth and elastic, 8 to 10 minutes. Place in a greased bowl, turning to grease top. Cover, let rise in a warm place, free from draft, until doubled in bulk, about 1 hour. Shape into loaves. Let rise again about 1/2 hour. Bake at 350° for 45 minutes.

Korpuja *(Finnish Cinnamon Toast)*

2 c. milk (scalded)
2 eggs
1/2 c. sugar
2 t. salt

1 pkg. dry yeast
1/2 t. ground cardamom (optional)
8 to 10 c. flour
1 stick oleo

Combine scalded milk (which has cooled to lukewarm), eggs, sugar, salt, oleo, and yeast which has been added to 1/2 c. lukewarm water. Add cardamom and 4 c. flour. Mix well, then add the rest of the flour to make a soft dough. Let rise for 2 hours. Divide dough in 4 equal parts, shape each portion into a roll (the length of a cookie sheet or jelly roll pan) and flatten with palm of hand to fill half the width of jelly roll pan. Let rise, covered with towel for 1 hour. Bake at 375° for 25 minutes.

Grease top, let cool, then cut into 1/2 inch slices. Spread lightly with melted butter (after arranging slices on cookie sheet). Sprinkle with mixture of sugar and cinnamon. Bake at 375° for 15 minutes. (Can be stored in dry paper bag after cooling completely.)

Raised Doughnuts

1 pkg. dry yeast	2 eggs (beaten)
1-1/2 c. lukewarm water	1 t. salt
2/3 c. shortening	2/3 c. sugar
1 c. hot mashed potatoes	7 to 7-1/2 c. flour (sifted)

Dissolve yeast in water. Add shortening, sugar, salt and eggs. Add mashed potatoes and work in flour with spoon. Raise dough, cut doughnuts and raise again. Fry in hot fat for 2 to 3 minutes. May be sugared or glazed while warm.

The center of raised doughnuts can be placed in greased muffin tins (3 or 4 in each) and baked. For caramel rolls place 1 t. melted butter and 1 t. brown sugar and 1 pecan in each muffin cup, place 3 or 4 doughnut centers on top. Bake.

Buns or Raised Doughnuts

1 c. milk (scalded)	1 c. lukewarm water
1/4 lb. oleo	6 c. flour
2 t. salt	1 egg
1 pkg. dry yeast	7 T. sugar
1 T. sugar	

Add oleo and salt to scalded milk. Let cool until lukewarm. In large bowl, mix water, yeast, and 1 T. sugar. Let stand about 10 minutes until the yeast is dissolved.

Add cooled milk and butter mixture. Add 3 c. of the unsifted flour and mix well. Add egg and 7 T. sugar. Add remaining 3 c. of flour. Mix well. Add 1/2 to 1 c. more flour, if necessary, to make stiff dough.

Turn onto floured board and knead until dough handles easily. Put dough into a greased bowl and let rise until double in size. Shape or cut for buns or doughnuts. Let rise 1 hour.

Bake buns in a 400° oven for 15 minutes or until brown. Fry doughnuts in hot deep fat.

Mart's Coffee Cake

1/2 c. shortening
3/4 c. sugar
1 t. vanilla
3 eggs

2 c. flour
1 t. baking powder
1 t. baking soda
1/2 pt. sour cream

TOPPING

6 T. butter
1 c. brown sugar

2 t. cinnamon
1 c. nuts

Cream shortening, sugar and vanilla. Add eggs, flour, baking powder, soda and sour cream. Spread half of batter on bottom of well greased tube pan (angel food cake pan). Dot batter with half of topping mixture. Cover with remaining batter. Top with remaining filling. Bake 50 minutes at 350°.

Finnish Kropsu *(Baked Pancake)*

3 eggs
1/2 c. sugar
1 t. salt
Preheat oven to 375°.

2 c. milk
1-1/4 c. flour
butter or margarine (melted)

Put all ingredients except butter into bowl. Beat with rotary beater until blended (will be very thin). Melt about 1/2 stick of butter in 9 x 13 inch pan. When butter is melted add about half of it to batter, leaving remaining butter in pan. Pour batter over hot butter and bake at 375° for 30 minutes. Will puff up while baking. Good served with syrup, jam, jelly or honey. Cut in squares to serve.

Pancakes or Waffles

2 c. buttermilk
2 c. flour
1 t. soda
1 t. baking powder

1/2 t. salt
1 T. sugar
4 T. shortening (melted)
2 eggs

Beat egg yolks until light. Sift all dry ingredients and add to yolks, beating with an electric beater, first adding a little buttermilk and then the dry ingredients, last the melted shortening. Beat the egg whites until stiff and fold in. Makes 6-7 large waffles.

Rieska

3 c. white flour	2 c. buttermilk
1-1/2 c. whole wheat or barley flour	1/4 c. sugar
3 t. baking powder	2 t. salt
1 t. baking soda	1/2 c. shortening

Mix as for pie crust. Flatten in ungreased pan. Bake at 350° about 25 minutes.

Potato Pancakes

2 c. raw potatoes (grated)	2 eggs
2 T. flour	1 t. salt
2 T. cream or milk	

Drain off excess water from grated potatoes. Add flour, cream, salt and beaten egg yolks. Fold in stiffly beaten egg whites. Drop by spoonful into frying pan after oil or shortening has been heated. Fry crisp and golden on one side, turn and fry other side. 4 servings.

Mixing Dough

I get more pleasure than you know
From mixing up a bit of dough;
A bowl of yellow edged in blue
Adds much to my enjoyment, too.

I sift the flour fresh and sweet
And vision fields of waving wheat,
Where singing winds of summer blow,
And toss the wheat, and bend it low;

I add a cup of measured cream
And then I see a shaded stream
With flowers growing by the brink
Where friendly cows come down to drink.

The eggs I beat, with all my might
Until I have a mound of white;
I hear the old hen as she sings,
And thank God for these common things.

Cakes and Frostings

Apple Pie Cake

3 c. flour
3 T. sugar
3 t. baking powder
1/4 t. salt

1 c. lard or shortening
3 eggs (beaten)
2 T. milk
apple pie filling

Sift dry ingredients together and add shortening; mix like pie crust. Beat eggs in separate bowl and add milk to eggs. Pour into flour mixture and mix to soft dough. Roll a bottom and top crust for 9 x 13 inch pan (greased). Put apple filling between as for pie. Bake at 350°, for 45 minutes or until nicely browned. Frost with thin, powdered sugar icing.

Chocolate Mayonnaise Cake

1 c. boiling water
1 c. mayonnaise
1 c. sugar

4 T. cocoa
2 c. cake flour
2 t. soda

Mix sugar and cocoa together. Mix boiling water and mayonnaise. Let cool 5 minutes. Add to sugar, cocoa mixture. Add flour and baking soda. Beat 2 minutes. Bake at 350° for 20-30 minutes.

Abigail's Pound Cake *(A Shaker Recipe)*

1 c. butter
1 c. sugar
5 eggs

1/2 t. rum flavoring
1/4 t. mace
2 c. all-purpose flour (sifted)

Cream butter well, add sugar gradually. After adding each egg, beat again! Add flavoring and gradually work in flour. Bake for 45 minutes in 350° oven. (No other liquid in recipe.)

Heath Bar Cake

2 c. brown sugar	1 egg
2 c. flour	1 c. milk
1/2 c. shortening	1 t. vanilla
1 t. soda	6-8 Heath bars
1/2 t. salt	1/2 c. nuts (chopped)

Mix sugar, flour and shortening, set 1 c. aside for topping. Preheat oven to 350°. Add to first mixture soda, salt, egg, milk, and vanilla. Pour into greased pan, sprinkle with remaining crumbs; then crush and sprinkle Heath bars and nuts over crumbs, and bake.

Pineapple Upside Down Cake

2-1/2 c. cake flour (sifted)	1 t. vanilla
3 t. baking powder	1 c. milk
1/4 t. salt	1/4 c. butter
1/2 c. shortening	1/2 c. brown sugar (packed)
1-1/2 c. granulated sugar	canned pineapple slices (drained)
2 eggs (well beaten)	maraschino cherries

Sift together flour, baking powder and salt. Cream shortening, gradually beat in sugar; mix well. Add eggs and vanilla; beat thoroughly. Add sifted dry ingredients alternately with milk. Melt 1/4 cup butter in a 12 inch skillet or similar size pan. Add brown sugar and spread evenly over pan. Arrange pineapple slices over sugar mixture with cherry in center of each. Pour cake batter over fruit. Bake about 40 minutes at 325°.

Danish Sand Cake

1 c. butter	3/4 c. potato starch flour
1 c. sugar	1 t. vanilla
3 whole eggs	1/2 t. lemon peel (grated)
3/4 c. flour	

Cream butter with sugar and add eggs, 1 at a time, beating well. Add sifted flour, vanilla and lemon peel. Pour into buttered loaf pan and bake in moderate oven, about 350° for 50 minutes to an hour.

Mayonnaise Cake

1 t. soda
1 c. hot water
1 c. dates (chopped)
1 t. vanilla
1/2 c. nuts (chopped)
2 c. flour

1 c. sugar
2 T. cocoa
1 t. cinnamon
1/2 t. salt
1 c. mayonnaise
whipped cream for topping

Combine soda, water and dates and let stand a few minutes. Sift dry ingredients and then stir together all ingredients. Bake in loaf pan at 350° for 40-50 minutes. Serve with whipped cream.

Red Velvet Cake

4 (1/2 oz.) bottles red food coloring
3 T. cocoa
1/2 c. shortening
1-1/2 c. sugar
2 eggs
1 c. buttermilk

2-1/4 c. flour
1/4 t. salt
1 t. vanilla
1 T. vinegar
1 t. baking soda

Mix food coloring and cocoa; let stand. Cream shortening with sugar, add eggs and coloring paste, blend well. Add buttermilk and flour with salt mixed in. Beat well. Add 1 t. vanilla. Remove from mixer. Add vinegar and baking soda; mix by hand. Pour into 2 well greased and floured 8 inch pans. Bake at 350° for 30-35 minutes.

Black Midnight Cake

1-2/3 c. sugar
2/3 c. soft shortening
3 eggs
2-1/4 c. flour
2/3 c. cocoa

1/4 t. baking powder
1-1/4 t. soda
1 t. salt
1-1/3 c. water
1 t. vanilla

Combine all ingredients (wet and dry). Beat until batter is smooth. Bake at 375° for about 30 minutes.

If you want to avoid being tempted to eat forbidden
fruit, stay out of the devil's orchard

White Pineapple Gumdrop Cake

1 c. shortening
2-1/2 c. sugar
3 eggs
1 t. salt
2-1/2 t. baking powder
1/2 t. almond extract
1/2 t. vanilla extract
1 c. coconut (fine)

1 c. pineapple juice
1 c. crushed pineapple
1/2 c. dates
1 c. nuts
1 c. raisins
1 lb. gumdrops (no black)
4 c. flour

Cream together shortening and sugar until fluffy; beat in eggs and extracts. Sift together flour, salt, and baking powder. Stir into egg mixture. Blend in gumdrops, raisins, nuts, dates, pineapple, pineapple juice and coconut. Fill prepared pans almost full. Bake 2-1/2 to 3 hours at 300°. Cover pans with paper the last hour. Store airtight in cool place.

Gumdrop Cake

2 c. shortening
1 c. white sugar
1 c. brown sugar
4 eggs (unbeaten)
4 c. flour
1 c. dates (cut)
1 c. walnuts
2 c. unsweetened applesauce

1/2 t. salt
2 t. cinnamon
2 t. nutmeg
2 t. soda
2 t. allspice
1 c. raisins
1 c. gumdrops (cut; no black ones)

Mix in order given. Bake in 3 greased loaf pans (may be lined with wax paper). Bake at 350° for 1 to 1-1/2 hours.

Peanut Butter Cake

1/2 c. smooth peanut butter
1/3 c. shortening
1-1/2 c. sugar
2 eggs (beaten)
1 t. vanilla

2 c. flour (sifted)
3 t. baking powder
1 t. salt
1/2 t. cinnamon
1 c. milk

Cream peanut butter, shortening and sugar. Add beaten eggs. Stir in vanilla. Add dry ingredients alternately with milk. Beat well. Pour into a 9 x 13 inch greased cake pan. Bake 45 minutes at 350° and cool. Frost with Cocoa Peanut Butter Frosting.

COCOA PEANUT BUTTER FROSTING

2 c. powdered sugar
1/3 c. cocoa
1/2 c. peanut butter

6 or 7 T. milk
1 t. vanilla

Sift powdered sugar with cocoa, add to peanut butter. Cream well while adding milk and vanilla. Spread on the cooled cake.

Chocolate Date and Nut Cake

1 small pkg. dates
1 c. boiling water
1 t. vanilla
1 T. cocoa
1-1/3 c. flour
1/2 c. chopped nuts

1 t. soda
1/2 c. shortening
1 c. sugar
2 eggs
1 c. chocolate chips

Mix dates, soda and water; set aside to cool. Cream shortening, sugar, eggs and vanilla. Sift cocoa and flour. Add to the creamed mixture. Add dates and balance of liquid, pinch of salt. Beat. Sprinkle chocolate chips and nuts on batter. Bake in moderate oven 30 minutes. Serve with whipped cream.

Jelly Roll

3 eggs
1 c. sugar
1 c. flour (sifted)
1 t. baking powder

1/4 t. salt
1/4 c. hot milk
1 t. vanilla

Separate eggs; beat yolks and whites separately. Then mix together and beat again. Add 1 c. sugar and beat; add 1 c. flour sifted with the baking powder and salt. Mix well. Lastly add the hot milk and vanilla. Spread in a cookie sheet which has been well greased and dusted with flour. Bake in a 400° oven for 10-12 minutes until done.

Have a towel spread out with wax paper on it on which you have sprinkled either powdered sugar or granulated sugar. Invert the cake on this as soon as you take it out of the oven. Take a knife and score the edges of the long side, thus making it easier to roll the cake. Then spread jelly, jam or lemon filling over cake. Roll it up beginning on the narrow side of the cake and leave it rolled up in the towel and wax paper for an hour or so before slicing.

Strawberry Cake

1 box white cake mix
1 (3 oz.) pkg. strawberry Jello
1/2 c. hot water

3/4 c. oil
4 eggs
1/2 c. frozen strawberries (thaw)

Mix together cake mix, Jello and water to make a stiff batter. Add oil, eggs and berries. Beat. Bake in a 9 x 13 inch pan for 40-50 minutes at 350°.

Chocolate Banana Cake

1/2 c. butter or margarine
1-1/2 c. brown sugar
2 eggs
1/3 c. mashed bananas
3 squares semi-sweet chocolate

1 t. vanilla
1 c. buttermilk
2 c. flour (sifted)
1 t. baking soda
1/2 t. salt

Cream butter and brown sugar; add eggs and beat until fluffy. Add mashed banana and melted chocolate and vanilla. Add sifted dry ingredients to creamed mixture, alternately with the buttermilk. Bake in 9 x 13 inch pan or 2 layer pans in 350° oven.

Apple Swirl Cake

1 c. walnuts (finely chopped)
1/2 c. sugar
1/2 c. butter or oleo
1 c. sugar
3 eggs
3 c. flour (sifted)
1 T. baking powder

1 t. salt
1 t. cinnamon
1 c. apple (grated)
3/4 c. dairy sour cream
1-1/2 c. apples (sliced)
1 T. butter or oleo

Combine walnuts and sugar and set aside. Cream butter and 1 c. sugar until fluffy. Beat in eggs, 1 at a time. Combine remaining dry ingredients and add to creamed mixture alternately with grated apple and sour cream, beating well. Spoon half of the batter into a well greased tube pan. Sprinkle with all but 2 T. of nut mixture. Cover with remaining batter. Arrange apple slices on top of batter. Sprinkle with remaining nuts, dot with 1 T. butter. Bake at 375° for 50 minutes or until done. Cool, then remove from pan.

Spicy Prune Cake

1 c. vegetable oil
1-1/2 c. sugar
3 eggs
2 c. flour (sifted)
1/2 t. salt
1 t. baking powder
1 t. baking soda

1 t. cinnamon
1 t. nutmeg
1 c. prunes (cooked, mashed)
1 c. buttermilk
1 c. pecans (chopped)
Caramel Glaze

Cream oil and sugar; add eggs, 1 at a time, beating well. Sift dry ingredients, add alternately to creamed mixture with prunes and buttermilk. Stir in pecans. Pour into greased and floured pan 9 x 13 inch; bake in moderate oven 350° for 35 minutes. Put pan on rack and pour hot Caramel Glaze over cake immediately.

CARAMEL GLAZE

Combine 1 c. sugar, 1/2 c. buttermilk, 1/2 t. baking soda, 1 T. corn syrup, 1/2 c. butter and 1/2 t. vanilla in medium sized saucepan. Bring to a rolling boil (over low heat) and boil 10 minutes, stirring occasionally. Pour over hot cake.

Carrot Cake

2 c. all-purpose flour
2 t. soda
2 t. cinnamon
1 t. salt
3 eggs (beaten)
2 c. sugar

1-1/2 c. oil
2 c. carrot (grated)
1 c. crushed pineapple (drained)
1 c. flaked coconut
1 c. nuts (chopped)
1 t. vanilla

Sift and combine dry ingredients. Combine and beat eggs, sugar, oil; add dry ingredients, then add carrot, pineapple, coconut, nuts and vanilla. Pour into greased and floured bundt pan (or 9 x 13 inch pan). Bake 1 hour at 350°.

Cream Cake

1 c. sweet cream
4 eggs
1 c. sugar
1/4 t. salt

3 t. baking powder
3-4 c. flour
vanilla

Combine first 4 ingredients and mix to blend, then 3 c. flour and baking powder. Mix in, then add more flour if necessary to make a nice mixture and add vanilla. Bake in oblong or two 9 inch layer cake pans until it springs back.

Coke Cake

Sift 2 c. flour and 2 c. sugar. In a saucepan put 1/2 c. butter, 1/2 cup Crisco oil, 3 T. cocoa, 1 c. Coca Cola. Bring to boil and pour over dry ingredients. Add 1 t. soda to 1/2 c. buttermilk. Add to mixture plus 1 T. vanilla. Add 2 beaten eggs and 1-1/2 c. miniature marshmallows. Mix well and bake at 350° for about 45 minutes, in well greased and floured pan, 10 x 15 inches or two 2 x 9 inch pans.

GLAZE TOPPING
1/4 c. butter
1-1/2 T. cocoa
3 T. Coke

1 t. vanilla
1 c. nuts (chopped; blender)

Mix and bring to boil. As soon as the cake comes out of the oven, prick holes all over the cake with a meat fork and pour topping over all. The cake should be made the day before cutting so the glaze is perfect. Do not take cake out of pan to frost. Leave in pan until ready to serve.

Chocolate Cake

1-2/3 c. flour
1-1/2 c. sugar
2/3 c. cocoa
1-1/2 t. soda
1/2 t. salt

1/2 c. oleo
1-1/2 c. buttermilk
1 t. vanilla
2 eggs

Combine all together, blend 1/2 minute on medium, then 3 minutes at high speed. Pour into 13 x 9 x 2 inch greased pan.

Brownie Sheet Cake and Frosting

1/2 c. oleo	2 eggs
3-1/2 T. cocoa	1 t. vanilla
1/2 c. Crisco (shortening)	1 t. salt
1 c. water	1 t. soda
2 c. flour (sifted)	1/2 c. buttermilk
2 c. sugar	

Bring first four ingredients (oleo, cocoa, Crisco, water) to a boil and set aside. Mix flour, sugar, eggs, vanilla, salt, soda, and buttermilk together. Add the boiled mixture to this and stir well. Pour into sheet pan 18 x 12 x 1 inch and bake at 400° for 20 minutes.

FROSTING

1/3 c. milk	1 lb. powdered sugar
1/2 c. oleo	1 t. vanilla
3-1/2 T. cocoa	1/2 c. nuts (chopped)
Dash of salt	

Start frosting 5 minutes before cake is done. Bring milk, oleo, cocoa and salt to a boil. Then add powdered sugar, vanilla and nuts. Stir well. Put frosting on cake as soon as it is done.

Rhubarb Pudding Cake

4 c. rhubarb (cut)	1 c. flour
1-2/3 c. sugar	1 t. baking powder
3/4 c. water	1/4 t. salt
1/3 shortening	2/3 c. milk
1 egg	1/2 t. vanilla

Combine rhubarb, 1 c. sugar, and water in saucepan. Cook over medium heat, stirring occasionally for 10 minutes (keep hot). Cream shortening with remaining sugar, add egg; beat until fluffy. Sift flour with baking powder and salt, add dry ingredients alternately with milk and vanilla. Turn into 2 layer pans, greased and floured. Carefully spoon hot sauce over batter. Chopped nuts may be sprinkled on top if desired. Bake at 350° for 35-40 minutes. 9 servings.

Two Egg Treasure Cake

SIFT TOGETHER:
2 c. flour
1-1/3 c. sugar
2-1/2 t. baking powder
3/4 t. salt

ADD:
1/2 c. shortening
1 t. vanilla
2/3 c. milk

Beat 2 minutes at medium speed. Add 2 eggs and 1/4 c. milk. Beat until smooth. Bake in a greased and floured 9 x 13 inch pan at 350° for 30 minutes.

Nutmeg Feather Cake

1/4 c. butter or oleo
1/4 c. shortening
1-1/2 c. sugar
1/2 t. vanilla
3 eggs (beaten)
2 c. all-purpose flour (sifted)

2 t. nutmeg
1 t. soda
1 t. baking powder
1/4 t. salt
1 c. buttermilk

Cream butter and shortening; gradually add sugar, creaming well. Add vanilla; add eggs; beat until light and fluffy. Sift dry ingredients, add to creamed mixture alternately with buttermilk. Pour into greased 9 x 13 inch pan, baking in moderate oven 350° for 35 to 40 minutes or until done. Sift confectioners' sugar over cake or frost when cool.

Creamy Walnut Cake

2 c. cake flour (sifted)
3 t. baking powder
1 t. salt
1/2 c. sugar
1 c. brown sugar
1/2 c. shortening

3/4 c. milk
2 eggs
1/4 c. milk
1/4 t. maple flavoring
1/3 c. nuts (finely chopped)

Sift together the flour, baking powder, salt, and sugar. Add the brown sugar, shortening, and milk. Mix enough to dampen flour. Beat 2 minutes at low speed. Add the eggs, milk, maple flavoring and walnuts. Beat 1 minute. Bake in 2 greased and floured 8 inch layer pans at 375° for about 25 minutes. Cool. Frost with Creamy Frosting. Decorate with walnuts.

CREAMY FROSTING

Cream 2 T. shortening with 2 T. butter. Add 1/8 t. salt. Beat in 1 egg yolk. Add 3-1/2 c. sifted confectioners' sugar alternately with 4-6 T. warm milk. Beat until smooth. Add 1 t. vanilla.

Orange Cake

1 orange
1 c. raisins
2 eggs (beaten)
1-1/4 c. sugar
1/2 c. shortening

1 t. soda
2 c. all-purpose flour
1/8 t. salt
3/4 c. sour milk
1 t. vanilla

Squeeze juice from orange and add 1/2 c. sugar to juice for the topping. Put orange and raisins through grinder. Cream shortening and sugar. Add beaten eggs and add sifted flour, salt, and soda with sour milk to creamed mixture. Add ground raisins and orange rind. Bake in greased flour pan 13 x 9-1/2 inches in oven 350° for 45 minutes. Spoon dissolved sugar and juice mixture over hot cake.

Gingerbread Layer Cake

Said to be Abraham Lincoln's favorite cake.

1 c. honey
1 t. ginger
1 t. cinnamon
1/2 t. ground cloves
2-1/4 c. all-purpose flour
1 t. baking powder

1 t. baking soda
1/2 t. salt
1/2 c. butter or margarine
1/2 c. brown sugar
1 egg
1-1/4 c. buttermilk

In small saucepan, heat honey and spices to boiling, remove from heat, cool. Sift together flour, baking powder, soda, and salt. In large mixer bowl, cream butter and sugar until fluffy. Gradually beat in honey mixture at high speed of mixer, add egg, mix thoroughly. Add flour mixture alternately with buttermilk, beating well after each addition. Pour into two 8 inch layer pans, bake in moderate oven, 350°, for 30-35 minutes. Cool completely and just before serving spread with whipped cream, using 1-1/2 c. whipping cream and 1 T. sugar. Sprinkle top layer with grated orange peel and 1 square grated semi-sweet chocolate.

Hot Milk Sponge Cake

SIFT:

1 c. flour   1 t. baking powder

BEAT:

3 eggs (about 10 minutes)

ADD:

1 c. sugar, gradually   2 t. lemon juice

Add 6 T. hot milk and flour mixture quickly. Pour mixture into ungreased tube pan. Bake at 350° for about 30-35 minutes.

Rhubarb Cake

2-1/2 c. brown sugar   3/4 c. shortening
1-1/2 c. sour milk   2-1/2 c. rhubarb
2 small eggs (beaten)   1-1/4 t. soda
3/4 t. salt   3 c. flour
2 t. vanilla

Mix sugar and shortening. Add eggs, vanilla and rhubarb (cut in thin slices). Mix soda and milk and add with flour and salt alternately. Pour in 9 x 13 inch pan. Top with the following mixture; bake at 350° for 1/2 hour or until done.

TOPPING

1/2 c. sugar   1/2 c. nuts, chopped
1-1/2 t. cinnamon

Butterscotch Chip Cake

1 c. brown sugar   1 t. vanilla
1/2 c. granulated sugar   1 c. buttermilk
1 t. baking soda   1/2 c. nuts (chopped)
2 c. flour   1 c. butterscotch chips
1/2 c. butter

Combine brown sugar, granulated sugar, soda, and flour. Cut in butter until particles are the size of cornmeal. Reserve 1/2 c. of this mixture. Add vanilla and buttermilk. Mix well. Pour into greased 9 x 13 inch pan. Add nuts to reserved mixture and sprinkle with butterscotch chips over batter. Bake at 350° for 35 minutes.

Fruit Cocktail Cake

1-1/2 c. flour (sifted)
1 c. sugar
1 c. brown sugar
1 t. soda

1/2 t. salt
1 egg (beaten)
2 c. fruit cocktail
whipping cream

Combine flour, sugar, soda and salt in mixing bowl. Beat in egg and juice from fruit cocktail, blend in fruit. Spread in greased 9 x 13 inch pan. Bake at 350° for 45 minutes. Serve warm with whipped cream. (May also reserve brown sugar for topping, mixing it with 3/4 c. chopped nuts and sprinkle on batter before baking.)

Molasses Cake

1/2 c. shortening
1/2 c. sugar
1/2 c. molasses
1 egg
1 c. sour milk
2-1/2 c. flour

1 t. soda
1 t. baking powder
1 t. salt
1/3 t. cinnamon
1/3 t. ginger
1/3 t. cloves

Mix in order given. Bake in 9 x 13 inch pan at 350° for 30 minutes.

Fresh Apple Cake

3 c. flour
2 c. sugar
3 eggs
1 t. each: vanilla, salt, soda, cinnamon

1-1/2 c. Wesson or Crisco oil
1 c. walnuts (chopped)
3 c. apples (diced)

Mix all ingredients and bake in preheated oven 350° for 30 minutes.

ICING

1 c. granulated sugar
1 c. evaporated milk
1 c. nuts (chopped)

1/4 lb. butter or margarine
2 T. flour

Mix flour and sugar and add rest of ingredients and boil about 10 minutes. Stir constantly. Pour warm icing over warm cake.

Wine Cake

1 pkg. yellow cake mix
1 regular size instant lemon pudding
3/4 c. cooking oil

3/4 c. light wine (sherry or sauterne)
4 eggs
1/4 t. nutmeg

Bake in greased bundt pan, 45 to 60 minutes in moderate oven, 350°. Cool cake before removing from pan. Sprinkle with powdered sugar. (A good keeping cake.)

Sour Cream Cheese Cake

2 (8 oz.) pkg. cream cheese
1-1/2 c. sour cream
1/2 c. sugar

2 eggs
1 t. vanilla
3 T. margarine or butter (melted)

In blender, put sour cream, sugar, eggs and blend until smooth (4-5 seconds). Add 1 inch squares of cream cheese as blender is running. Blend 15 to 20 seconds or until smooth. Add vanilla and butter. Blend a few more seconds. Pour into a deep graham cracker crust. Bake in a 10 inch pie pan at 350° for 45 minutes or until center is firm.

Peach Spice Pudding Cake

1 pkg. lemon pie filling (not instant)
1 No. 303 can sliced peaches (drained)

1 box honey spice cake mix

Prepare lemon pie filling and spread in oblong pan. Arrange drained peach slices over pudding. Add mixed cake batter over peaches. Bake about 50 minutes at 350°. Serve warm, cut in squares and turn upside down.

Easy Peach and Butter Brickle Cake

2 cans sliced peaches
1 pkg. Butter Brickle cake mix

1 c. nuts (chopped)
1-1/3 sticks oleo (melted)

Put peaches in bottom of 9 x 13 inch pan with enough of the syrup from peaches to cover the pan about 1/4 inch. Sprinkle dry cake mix over peaches, sprinkle nuts on top of mix. Spoon melted oleo or butter on top. Bake for 40-45 minutes, at 375°.

Date-Loaf Cake

2-1/4 c. white sugar
1-1/2 T. shortening
2 eggs
1 T. vanilla
2-1/4 c. boiling water

3 t. soda
1 pkg. dates (cut fine)
4-1/2 c. flour (about)
1/2 t. salt
1 c. nuts (chopped)

Pour water over dates, add soda and let stand overnight. Mix sugar, shortening, eggs, vanilla, and nuts. Add date mixture, then add flour and salt. Makes 3 loaf pans. Grease pans well, and line with wax paper. Bake 350° for 1/2 hour, then lower to 300° for 1/2 hour.

Chocolate Sauerkraut Cake

1-1/2 c. sugar
2/3 c. oleo
3 eggs
1 t. vanilla
1 c. water
2-1/4 c. flour

1/2 c. cocoa
1 t. baking powder
1 t. soda
1/4 t. salt
2/3 c. chopped sauerkraut
    (rinsed, drained)

Cream well the sugar and oleo. Add and beat thoroughly the eggs and vanilla. Add water and dry ingredients alternately with above creamed mixture. Add sauerkraut last. Bake in 9 x 12 inch pan or sheet for 35-40 minutes at 350°.

ICING

4 T. butter or margarine
3 c. powdered sugar
4 squares chocolate (melted)

1/3 c. milk
1 t. vanilla

Warm milk and add to sugar. Add chocolate and margarine and vanilla and beat 5 minutes with mixer. Spread on warm cake.

It is one of the most beautiful compensations of this life that no man can sincerely try to help another without helping himself.

Dream Cake

1 pkg. (2 layer size) yellow, white or chocolate cake mix 4 eggs
1 envelope Dream Whip topping mix (not whipped) 1 c. cold water

Combine all ingredients in large bowl of mixer. Blend until moistened. Beat at medium speed for 4 minutes. Pour into 2 greased and floured 9 x 5 inch loaf pans. Bake at 350° for 45 minutes. Cool in pan 10 minutes. Remove and finish cooling on racks. Dream Cake can be baked in other size pan as 1 tube cake pan. Bake 45 to 50 minutes.

Chocolate Walnut Loaf

1 c. butter or margarine   2-1/2 c. cake flour (sifted)
2 c. sugar   1 t. baking soda
5 eggs (well beaten)   1/4 t. salt
2 squares unsweetened chocolate   1 c. buttermilk
1 t. vanilla   1 c. walnuts (chopped)

Cream butter, add sugar; add eggs and melted chocolate. Blend. Add vanilla. Add sifted dry ingredients alternately with buttermilk. Fold in nuts. Pour into 2 greased loaf pans 8 x 4 x 2 inches. Bake in slow oven 325° for 1 hour. Makes 2 cakes. Frost or sprinkle with powdered sugar.

Blue Ribbon Fruitcake

3 c. all-purpose flour (sifted)   1/2 c. milk
1 t. baking powder   1/2 c. apple jelly (softened)
1 t. salt   1 lb. candied cherries
1/2 lb. butter or margarine   1 lb. candied pineapple
1-1/2 c. sugar   1-1/2 c. light raisins
4 eggs   3 c. walnuts or pecans (broken)

Sift together flour, baking powder and salt. Cream together butter, and sugar. Add eggs, 1 at a time beating just until mixed. Stir in softened jelly, add sifted dry ingredients alternately with milk. Pour batter over remaining ingredients, mixing well. Bake in 9 inch tube pan that has been greased and lined with foil. Bake at 275° for about 3 hours. Place 2 c. of water in a pan on bottom of oven shelf while baking. Cool in pan on rack. Makes a 6 lb. cake. Will keep indefinitely when well wrapped in foil and refrigerated. I have kept it over a year with no change in flavor.

Lemon-Jello Cake

1 box lemon Jello
1 c. boiling water
1 box yellow cake mix
3/4 c. oil

4 eggs
2 t. lemon extract
Glaze

Dissolve Jello in boiling water. Let jell until consistency of unbeaten egg white. Mix cake mix, eggs (one at a time), oil and lemon extract. Add Jello mix. Pour into greased, floured tube pan. Bake 1 hour at 350°.

GLAZE

2 c. powdered sugar
2 t. lemon extract

About 1 c. lemon juice

Mix and pour on warm cake. Let stand 30 minutes, remove from pan.

Blueberry Cake

CREAM TOGETHER:
1/2 c. oleo or margarine
1 c. sugar

ADD:
3 eggs, beaten
1 c. sour cream

SIFT TOGETHER AND BLEND IN:
1-3/4 c. flour
1 t. soda
1/2 t. salt

Fold in 2 c. fresh blueberries dusted with flour. Spread half the batter in 13 x 9 greased pan. Sprinkle with 1/2 c. brown sugar and 1/2 t. cinnamon. Spread rest of batter on top. Bake at 350° for 50 minutes.

White Cake

1/2 c. shortening
1-1/2 c. sugar
2 c. cake flour
2 t. baking powder

1/4 t. salt
1 c. milk
2 eggs
1 t. vanilla

Very important: Mix dry ingredients in bowl. Add 3/4 c. milk. Mix for 2 minutes. Add eggs, 1/4 c. milk and vanilla. Beat for 1 minute. Put in pan and bake in 375° oven for 35 minutes.

Princess Peach Cake

2 c. flour	1/2 c. pure peach preserves
1 t. soda	1/2 c. orange juice
1 t. salt	1 t. orange rind (grated)
1-1/4 c. sugar	1/4 c. water
1 t. cinnamon	2 eggs
1/2 c. margarine	1/2 c. nuts (chopped)

Sift dry ingredients together into a mixing bowl. Cut in margarine and add preserves, juice, rind and water. Beat, adding eggs, until well blended. Stir in nuts, pour into greased 9 x 13 inch pan. Bake at 350° oven 40 minutes; cool and frost.

PEACH FROSTING

1/3 c. margarine	1/2 c. peach preserves
3 c. confectioners' sugar (sifted)	

Cream margarine and add sugar alternately with peach preserves. Beat until light and fluffy.

Navy Cake

1 c. vegetable oil	1/2 c. cocoa
1 c. hot water	2 c. sugar
1 c. buttermilk	2 c. flour
2 eggs	1 t. salt
1 t. vanilla	2 t. soda

Mix all dry ingredients in large bowl. Add liquids, mix well, pour into ungreased loaf pan. Bake at 350° for 45 minutes. During last 15 minutes of baking prepare icing:

ICING

In small saucepan, put 1 c. sugar, 3 T. cornstarch, 1 oz. unsweetened chocolate, 1/4 t. salt. Mix well, then add 3 T. oleo and 1 c. boiling water. Cook to thick pudding. Pour over cake as soon as it comes out of the oven.

Blueberry Cake

2 c. sugar
1/2 c. Crisco
3 eggs
1/2 c. sour milk or buttermilk
1 t. baking soda
2 t. baking powder

MIX WITH:
3 c. flour
1 t. salt
1 t. mace
2 c. blueberries

Turn into 2 greased loaf pans and bake 45 minutes in 350° oven. When warm, brush with melted butter and sprinkle with sugar.

Coconut Cupcakes

1-3/4 c. flour
2-1/2 t. baking powder
1/2 t. salt
1 c. sugar
2/3 c. shortening

2/3 c. milk
1 t. vanilla
3 eggs
1 c. shredded coconut

Sift dry ingredients in a mixing bowl. Add shortening, milk, and vanilla. Beat vigorously with a spoon for 2 minutes (about 150 strokes per minute), or with a mixer 2 minutes at low speed. Add unbeaten eggs and beat again for 2 minutes. Stir in coconut. Spoon into well greased muffin pans. Bake at 375° for 25-30 minutes. Yield is 20-24 cupcakes.

Applesauce Cupcakes *(Different!)*

1 c. sugar
1/2 c. shortening
1/2 c. milk
2-1/2 c. flour (all-purpose)
2 t. cream of tartar

1 egg
1 t. soda
1 t. vanilla
1 can applesauce

Mix as for cake, except heat applesauce in saucepan. Put batter into cupcake pans, pushing batter to sides and leaving an indentation in the center of each cupcake. Spoon warm applesauce into center and bake for 12 to 15 minutes at 400°. Batter bakes up and applesauce gets left inside cupcakes. Nice surprise to eat.

Truly Different Cupcakes

4 squares semi-sweet chocolate
2 sticks margarine
1/4 t. butter flavoring
1-1/2 c. broken pecans

1-3/4 c. sugar
1 c. unsifted flour
4 large eggs
1 t. vanilla

Melt the margarine and chocolate squares in a saucepan. Add butter flavoring. Stir. Add the pecans and mix until well coated.

In a separate bowl, add all other ingredients. Mix but do not beat! Add chocolate-nut mixture to remaining ingredients and blend thoroughly. Again, do not beat! Pour into paper baking cups, fill 1/2 full (or just a little more.) Batter will be thin and runny.

Bake at 325° for 30 minutes. Watch carefully the last 5 minutes of baking to prevent burning. Yield: 18 to 20 cupcakes.

Harvest Loaf Cake

1-3/4 c. flour (sifted)
1 t. soda
1 t. cinnamon
1/2 t. salt
1/2 t. nutmeg
1/4 t. ginger
1/4 t. ground cloves

1/2 c. butter
1 c. sugar
2 eggs
3/4 c. canned or cooked pumpkin
3/4 c. chocolate chips
3/4 c. walnuts (chopped—reserve 1/4 c.)

Oven 350°. Grease bottom of 9 x 5 inch loaf pan. Combine flour with soda, salt, and spices. Cream butter, add sugar and cream well. Blend in eggs, beat well at low speed. Add dry ingredients alternately with pumpkin beginning and ending with dry ingredients. Stir in chocolate chips and walnuts. Turn into prepared pan. Sprinkle with 1/4 c. walnuts. Bake for 65-75 minutes. Cool. Drizzle with glaze. Let stand 6 hours before cutting.

SPICE GLAZE

Combine 1/2 c. powdered sugar, 1/8 t. nutmeg, and 1/8 t. cinnamon. Blend in 1-2 T. cream. Cream until right consistency.

A good rule for talking is one used in
measuring flour: <u>sift</u> <u>first</u>.

Canadian War Cake

2 c. brown sugar
2 c. hot water
4 T. lard
1 c. raisins

1 t. salt
1/2 t. cloves
1 t. cinnamon

Boil for 5 minute all the above ingredients. Cool and add 3 c. flour and 2 t. soda in small amount of hot water. Bake 300° for 40 minutes.

Never-Fail Chocolate Cake

2 c. sugar
2 eggs
1/4 c. shortening
1 T. vinegar
2 t. baking soda
1 c. fresh, sour or buttermilk

1 t. vanilla
2-1/2 c. flour
1/2 t. salt
9 T. cocoa
1 c. boiling water

Cream together sugar and shortening; add eggs. Mix well. Combine vinegar, soda, milk, and vanilla; add to first mixture. Sift together flour, salt, and cocoa; blend into other ingredients. Add boiling water. Bake in 9 x 13 inch pan at 375° for 35 minutes.

Toll House Cupcakes

1/2 c. soft butter
6 T. granulated sugar
6 T. brown sugar
1/2 t. vanilla

1 egg
1 c. plus 2 T. flour
1/2 t. baking soda
1/2 t. salt

FILLING

1/2 c. brown sugar
1 egg
1/8 t. salt

6 oz. chocolate chips
1/2 t. vanilla
1/2 c. nuts (chopped)

Cream butter, sugars and vanilla. Beat in egg. Stir in dry ingredients. Spoon by rounded T. into paper-lined cupcake pans. Bake at 375° for 10-12 minutes.

Prepare filling—Combine brown sugar, egg, and salt. Stir in remaining ingredients. Spoon 1 T. over each cupcake. Return to oven and bake at 375° for 15 minutes.

Raisin Cupcakes

3/4 c. brown sugar
1/2 c. shortening
1 egg
1 t. vanilla
1 t. soda

1/4 t. salt
1-1/2 c. flour
1/2 cup raisin liquid
1 c. cooked raisins

Boil raisins for 15 minutes. Cool and strain. Beat sugar and shortening. Add egg and vanilla; beat again. Dissolve soda in raisin water and add alternating with flour and salt. Flour raisins lightly and fold in last. Drop in paper lined cupcake tins and bake in 350° oven for 25 minutes. Makes 18 cupcakes.

Quick Sponge Cake

4 eggs
1 c. sugar

1 c. flour
1/8 t. salt

Beat eggs, sugar and salt for 20 minutes at high speed. Fold in flour. Pour into sponge cake pan and bake for 1 hour at 375°.

Chocolate Frosting

1 c. sugar
1/4 c. milk
1/4 c. butter

1/2 c. chocolate chips
1 t. vanilla

Combine sugar, milk and butter in saucepan. Stir until boiling. Boil 1 minute. Add chips and vanilla. Beat until smooth and fairly thick. Spread on cake.

Icing

3 T. red fruit flavored gelatin
1 small egg white
1/2 c. sugar

1/8 t. cream of tartar
2 T. water

Place ingredients into double boiler over boiling water, beat until icing holds stiff peaks. Remove from heat and beat 1 minute longer.

Fluffy Frosting

1 c. cold milk	1/2 c. Crisco
5 T. flour	1 c. sugar
1/2 c. oleo	1 t. vanilla

Mix milk and flour until blended. Cook until thick. Cool. Mix together oleo, Crisco, sugar, and vanilla. Beat until smooth, then add flour mixture. Beat until it forms stiff peaks.

Custard Frosting

(A not-too-sweet frosting. Excellent for very-rich cakes.)

1 egg	1/2 c. sugar
2 T. flour	1 c. milk
1 t. vanilla	1/2 lb. sweet butter

In top of double boiler, mix together sugar, flour, beaten egg. Bring to a boil, stirring constantly, until thick. Cool. Cream butter with electric mixer until fluffy. Add cool custard slowly and beat with mixer 20 minutes. (Cake frosted with this frosting must be kept in refrigerator.)

Fluffy Frosting

1 c. sugar	1 egg
1/2 c. butter	1/3 c. milk
1/2 c. shortening	1 t. vanilla

Scald milk and cool and add over other ingredients. Whip with electric beater for 15 minutes.

Sander's Frosting

1/2 c. butter	1/2 c. shortening
1 c. white sugar	1/2 to 2/3 c. hot milk

Combine sugar with butter and margarine. Beat with mixer until sugar is gone. Keep milk hot to dissolve sugar. Add milk and vanilla. Beat to desired consistency.

Decorators' Frosting

1/4 c. white sugar
2 T. water
2 egg whites (stiffly beaten)

2/3 c. vegetable shortening
1 t. vanilla
1 lb. powdered sugar

Boil sugar and water 1 minute. Pour over the stiffly beaten whites of 2 eggs. Add shortening, vanilla, and powdered sugar. Beat until fluffy. Makes enough to frost 8 or 9 inch layer cake. (May be used for making roses by adding a little more powdered sugar.)

Good Cookie Frosting

Melt 1 c. of chocolate chips over hot water; when melted remove from heat. Add 1/2 c. commercial sour cream.

Double Boiler Icing

1 egg white
3/4 c. sugar
1/8 t. cream of tartar

3 T. water
1/2 t. vanilla

Mix in top of double boiler. Place over boiling water and beat with rotary beater until mixture holds its shape. Fold in vanilla. Remove from over hot water, beat until stiff.

Minute-Boil Fudge Frosting

1-1/2 c. sugar
2 squares chocolate
1 T. syrup
1/4 t. salt

2 T. shortening
2 T. oleo
7 T. milk
1 t. vanilla

Combine ingredients (except vanilla) in heavy saucepan. Bring slowly to a boil, stirring constantly. Boil 1 minute. Remove from heat. Add vanilla. Let cool. Beat until of right consistency to spread.

Favorite Chocolate Frosting

6 T. milk
6 T. butter or oleo
1/2 t. vanilla

1-1/2 c. sugar
3/4 c. chocolate chips

Bring milk, butter and sugar to a rolling boil. Boil 1/2 minute (no longer). Remove from heat and add chocolate chips and vanilla. Stir until smooth.

Vanilla Pudding Frosting

1 envelope whipped topping mix
(Dream Whip)
1 pkg. vanilla instant pudding mix

1-1/2 c. cold milk
1 t. vanilla extract

In a chilled deep bowl, blend and whip topping mix, pudding mix, cold milk and vanilla until stiff (3 to 8 minutes.) Immediately frost cake. Store cake in refrigerator.

Easy Frosting

1 (6 oz.) can frozen orange or
    pineapple concentrate

1 c. heavy cream
Sugar (to taste)

Place frozen concentrate in bowl; add cream and whip until it mounds, then add sugar to taste. Very good served on angel or spice cake.

Caramel Icing

2 c. brown sugar
1/2 c. butter

1/2 c. sweet cream
1 t. vanilla

Combine all ingredients except vanilla. Boil 5 minutes (no longer), beat until creamy, adding vanilla. Spread on cake.

The Cookie Jar

You can rig up a house with all manner of things,
The prayer rugs of sultans and princes and kings;
You can hang on its walls the old tapestries rare
Which some dead Egyptian once treasured with care;
But though costly and gorgeous its furnishings are,
It must have, to be homelike, an old cookie jar.

There are just a few things that a home must possess,
Besides all your money and all your success:
A few good old books which some loved one has read,
Some trinkets of those whose sweet spirits have fled,
And then in the pantry, not shoved back too far
For the hungry to get to, that old cookie jar.

Let the house be a mansion, I care not at all!
Let the finest of pictures be hung on each wall,
Let the carpets be made of the richest velour,
And the chairs only those which great wealth can procure,
I'd still want to keep for the joy of my flock
That homey, old-fashioned, well-filled cookie crock.

Like the love of the Mother it shines through our years;
It has soothed all our hurts and has dried away tears;
It has paid us for toiling; in sorrow or joy,
It has always shown kindness to each girl and boy;
And I'm sorry for people, whoever they are,
Who live in a house where there's no cookie jar.

Edgar A. Guest

Cookies and Bars

Sour Cream Cookies

2 c. sugar
1 c. butter (1/2 oleo)
1 c. thick sour cream
2 eggs

1/2 t. nutmeg
1 t. soda
3-1/2 to 4 c. flour

Mix in general order. If dough is soft it may be dropped from spoon on baking sheet (it may be rolled and cut with cutter if desired.) Bake at 375° for 8 to 10 minutes. Watch closely as they scorch easily.

Chocolate Nougat Cookies

4 eggs
1 c. granulated sugar
2 T. baking powder
1-1/2 c. flour (less 1 T.)

1/4 t. salt
1 lb. dates
1 lb. walnuts
1 t. vanilla

Beat eggs and sugar well, add sifted flour, salt, and baking powder. Add dates, nuts and vanilla. Put in 2 well greased loaf pans and bake 325° for 1 hour. When done, remove from pans, cool and wrap in wax paper. Store in cold place for 3 to 4 hours.

Cut into thin slices, then into half slices and dip in chocolate and cool on wax paper.

DIPPING CHOCOLATE
2 lb. sweet chunk chocolate   1 square of paraffin wax
Shave for faster melting. Melt in double boiler. Mix well and dip cookies. Lay on wax paper to cool.

Melting Moments

1/2 c. cornstarch
1/2 c. confectioners' sugar

1 c. flour (sifted)
3/4 c. margarine

Sift cornstarch, sugar and flour together into mixing bowl. Blend in margarine with spoon, mixing until a soft, smooth dough forms. Pinch off dough to form 1 inch balls. Place about 1-1/2 inches apart on ungreased cookie sheet. Flatten lightly with floured fork. Bake 300° slow oven until edges are lightly browned, 20-25 minutes. Makes about 3 dozen.

Fat Raisin Cookies

2 c. raisins
1 c. water
1 c. butter
2 c. sugar
3 eggs
1-1/2 t. cinnamon
4 c. flour

1/4 t. nutmeg
1 t. baking soda
1 t. baking powder
1/4 t. allspice
2 t. salt
1 t. vanilla
1 c. nutmeats (chopped)

Boil 2 c. raisins and 1 c. water 5 minutes and cool. Mix butter, sugar, and eggs and beat well. Sift dry ingredients and add to butter mixture. Alternately with raisins and liquid, add vanilla and nutmeats. Drop rounded t. on greased cookie sheet. Bake 15 minutes at 400°. Makes about 6 to 7 dozen.

Jelly Centers

1-1/2 c. white sugar
1 egg
1/4 stick butter or oleo
1/2 c. milk
3 c. white flour (sifted)

1 t. salt
1 t. baking soda
1 t. baking powder
1 small jar grape jelly

Sift sugar into large mixing bowl, mix in softened butter or oleo with spoon. Break egg into mixture and mix well. Put milk in slowly, only half. Then sift flour, salt, soda, and baking powder together over the other mixture and stir until quite firm, then add rest of milk. Use a T. to make rounded shapes of dough and then dent the center in with a small spoon. Then place on a greased cookie sheet, fill centers with jelly and bake in oven at 350° for 12 to 15 minutes.

Toffee Crunch Cookies

1-1/2 c. flour (sifted)
1/2 t. baking soda
1/2 t. salt
1/2 c. butter
3/4 c. brown sugar (packed)

1 egg
1 t. vanilla
1 c. Heath English toffee candy
   bars (finely chopped)
1/3 c. pecans (coarsely chopped)

Combine flour, soda, and salt. Cream butter. Add sugar, egg, and vanilla. Mix until creamy. Stir in dry ingredients. Blend in candy bars and pecans. Drop by T. 2 inches apart on greased baking sheets. Bake in moderate oven 350° for 12 to 15 minutes. Yields about 3 dozen cookies.

Snow Flake Cookies

1 c. shortening
1 (3 oz.) pkg. cream cheese
1 c. sugar
1 egg yolk
1 t. orange rind

2-1/2 c. flour
1/2 t. salt
1 t. vanilla
1/4 t. cinnamon

Cream shortening and cheese. Add sugar gradually and continue creaming. Beat egg yolk, vanilla, cinnamon and orange rind. Add to creamed mixture; add flour and salt. Bake at 350° for 12 to 15 minutes.

Chocolate Chip Drop Cookies

1 c. brown sugar
1/2 c. shortening
1/4 c. boiling water
1-1/2 c. flour (sifted)
1 c. chocolate chips
1 c. coconut
1 t. vanilla

1/2 c. white sugar
2 eggs (beaten)
Add 1/2 t. soda to water
1 c. quick cooking oatmeal
1 c. Kellogg's K
1/2 c. walnuts

Cream shortening and sugar. Add eggs, and water-soda mixture. Stir in flour and oatmeal. Add vanilla, chips, K, coconut and nuts. Let chill in refrigerator 1 hour. Form into balls and press with a fork. Bake in a preheated 400° oven for 10 to 12 minutes. Makes 6 dozen.

Refrigerator Date Pinwheels

FILLING

2-1/4 c. pitted dates	1 c. water
1 c. white sugar	1 c. nuts (chopped)

Combine dates, sugar and water; cook over low heat until thick, about 10 minutes. Then add nuts and cool.

COOKIES

1 c. shortening (oleo)	4 c. all-purpose flour (sifted)
2 c. brown sugar	1/2 t. salt
3 eggs (beaten)	1/2 t. baking soda

While dates are cooling, cream shortening. Add brown sugar gradually while creaming. Add well beaten eggs and beat well. Add remaining ingredients sifted together and mix well. Chill thoroughly.

Divide mixture in 2 parts and roll each out separately into a rectangle, a little less than 1/4 inch thick. Spread each with date filling and roll up as for jelly roll into 2 longs rolls. Chill thoroughly, at least overnight. Then cut with sharp knife into slices about 1/4 inch thick. Bake at 400° oven for 10-12 minutes.

Applesauce Bars

1/3 c. butter or margarine	1/2 t. cloves
1 c. sugar	1/2 t. cinnamon
1 egg	1/2 t. nutmeg
2 c. flour	1 c. applesauce
1/2 t. soda	1 c. raisins
1/2 t. salt	1 c. nuts (chopped)

Cream butter and sugar. Add egg and beat well. Mix dry ingredients and add alternately with applesauce, to first mixture. Add raisins and nuts. Spread in greased jelly roll pan, 15 x 10 x 2 inch. Bake 20-25 minutes at 375°. Cut in bars. Cool in pan before removing.

Thought—Real love is helping someone who can't return the favor.

Almond Crescents

1 c. butter
1/2 c. sugar
1 t. almond extract
confectioners' sugar

Red and green colored sugar
2 c. flour
1/2 t. salt
3/4 c. almonds (finely chopped)

Cream butter and sugar; beat in almond extract. Add flour and salt. Mix well. Stir in nuts; chill. Shape rounded t. of dough into crescents; place on ungreased cookie sheets. Bake 325° for 15 to 20 minutes. Sprinkle with confectioners' sugar or colored sugar. Makes 5 dozen cookies.

Chocolate Chip Cookies

2-1/4 c. flour
1 t. baking soda
1 t. salt
1 c. oleo
2 eggs
3/4 c. brown sugar

3/4 c. granulated sugar
1 t. vanilla
1/2 t. water
2 c. chocolate chips
1 c. nuts (optional)

Sift together flour, soda, and salt. Blend oleo, sugars, vanilla and water. Beat in eggs. Add flour mixture. Mix thoroughly. Stir in chocolate chips and nuts. Drop by spoon on greased sheet. Bake for 10 to 12 minutes.

Honey Nut Drops

3 c. flour (sifted)
4 t. baking powder
1/2 t. salt
1 T. cinnamon
1 c. butter or oleo

1 c. brown sugar (firmly packed)
1 c. honey
1 egg
3 c. nuts (chopped)

Sift flour, add baking powder, salt, and cinnamon and sift again. Cream butter with brown sugar until light and fluffy. Add honey gradually, beating well. Add egg and beat thoroughly. Add dry ingredients gradually beating until smooth. Fold in nuts. Chill 1 hour. Drop by level t. on greased baking sheets. Bake at 350° for 8 to 10 minutes. Cool on wire racks. Makes 65 cookies, 2 inches in diameter.

The greatest calamity is not to have failed; but to have failed to try.

Lumberjack Cookies

1/2 c. white sugar	1 t. vanilla
1 c. brown sugar	1 c. canned milk
1/2 c. butter or oleo	2-3/4 c. flour (or as needed)
2 eggs	1/2 t. soda

Mix in general order; chill dough; drop by spoon on greased cookie sheet. Bake at 350°. While warm frost with following:

2 T. melted butter	1/4 c. evaporated milk
2 c. confectioners' sugar	vanilla

Whole Peanut Cookies

1 c. butter	1/2 c. crushed corn flakes
1 c. brown sugar	1-1/4 c. quick cook oatmeal
1 egg	1 c. whole salted peanuts
1-1/2 c. flour	1-1/4 t. soda
1-1/4 t. baking powder	

Cream butter, add brown sugar gradually, cream well. Add egg, beat well. Sift flour, soda, baking powder together. Fold dry ingredients into creamed mixture. Add corn flakes, oatmeal, and peanuts. Form into balls about the size of walnuts. Place on greased cookie sheet. Bake at 350° for about 15 minutes. Yield: 4-1/2 dozen.

Molasses Praline Bars

1/4 c. butter	1/2 t. salt
1/2 c. sugar	1-1/2 t. vanilla
1/4 c. molasses	1-1/2 c. nuts
1 egg	3/4 c. flour

Melt butter in saucepan; blend in sugar and molasses. Add egg, salt, vanilla and beat well. Stir in nuts and flour. Pour into greased and floured 11 x 7 inch baking pan. Bake at 350° for 30 minutes. Cool slightly, cut into bars. (Double recipe for jelly roll pan.)

Seven-Layer Cookies

1/4 lb. oleo (melted)
1 c. graham cracker crumbs
1 c. flaked coconut (optional)
1 (6 oz.) pkg. chocolate chips

1 (6 oz.) pkg. butterscotch chips
1 can sweetened condensed milk
1 c. nuts

Place melted butter in 13 x 9 inch pan; add ingredients in layers in order as listed. Bake 30 minutes in 350° oven. Let cool in pan; cut into squares. Yield: 24-30 servings.

Sugar 'N' Spice Cookies

MIX TOGETHER:
3/4 c. shortening
1 c. sugar
1 egg
1/4 c. molasses

SIFT TOGETHER:
2 c. flour
2 t. soda
1/4 t. salt
1 t. cinnamon
3/4 t. cloves
3/4 t. ginger

Form into balls, the size of walnuts. Bake 10 to 12 minutes at 375°. Roll in powdered sugar while still warm. Makes 4 to 5 dozen cookies.

Peanut Butter Bars

1/2 c. butter
1/2 c. sugar
1/2 c. brown sugar
1 egg
1/3 c. peanut butter

1/2 t. soda
1/4 t. vanilla
1 c. flour
1 c. oatmeal

Mix all ingredients together. Spread in greased 9 x 13 inch pan. Bake at 350° for 20-25 minutes. After done baking sprinkle 1 c. chocolate chips on top and let stand 5 minutes. Pour following over chocolate chips:

COMBINE:
1/2 c. powdered sugar
1/4 c. peanut butter

2-4 T. milk

Peanut Butter Chews

1/3 c. shortening
1/2 c. peanut butter
1 c. sugar
1/4 t. salt
1 t. vanilla

1 egg
1 c. flour (sifted)
1 t. baking powder
1 c. shredded coconut

Combine shortening, peanut butter, sugar, salt, vanilla, and egg. Sift flour with baking powder and add to first mixture. Add coconut. Put in 9 x 13 inch pan. Bake at 350° for 25 to 30 minutes. Cut in strips while warm, sprinkle with or roll in powdered sugar.

Dad's Cookies

1 c. shortening
1 c. brown sugar
1 egg (beaten)
1 t. vanilla
1 c. coconut

1 c. oatmeal
1-3/4 c. flour
1/2 t. soda
1/2 t. baking powder

Cream together the shortening, brown sugar, egg and vanilla. Add the dry ingredients. Roll into small balls and flatten with a glass with a moistened cloth held tightly over the end. Bake about 10 minutes at 375°.

Raisin Filled Cookies

2 c. brown sugar
1 c. shortening (oleo)
3 eggs

1 t. each: soda, salt, vanilla
4 c. flour (use more when rolled)

FILLING

1 c. ground raisins
  (dates can be used)
1 T. flour

1 c. brown sugar
1 c. water

Filling—Cook and let cool before using.

Dough—Roll thin before putting filling between.

Mincemeat Bars

1/2 c. margarine (softened)
1 c. brown sugar
2 eggs (beaten)
1 t. vanilla
1 c. prepared mincemeat
Confectioners' sugar

1-1/2 c. flour
1/2 t. baking powder
1/2 t. salt
1/4 t. soda
1/2 c. nuts (chopped)

Cream margarine and sugar. Blend in eggs and vanilla. Sift together flour, baking powder, salt and soda. Add alternately with mincemeat, mixing well after each addition. Stir in nuts. Pour into greased and floured 9 inch square baking pan. Bake at 350° for 40-45 minutes. Cool, sift confectioners' sugar over top. Cut into 2 inch bars. Makes 20 bars.

Rhubarb Bars

FILLING
3 c. cut rhubarb
1-1/2 c. sugar
2 T. cornstarch
1/4 c. water
1 t. vanilla
1/2 t. soda

BASE
1-1/2 c. oatmeal
1 c. brown sugar
1 c. margarine
1/2 c. walnuts (chopped)
1-1/2 c. flour

To prepare filling—Mix cornstarch with sugar and add to rest of ingredients and simmer until thick. Set aside.

Mix the base ingredients until crumbly. Pat 3/4 of mixture into a 9 x 13 inch pan. Pour on cooked rhubarb filling and sprinkle remaining crumbs over top. Bake at 375° for 30-35 minutes.

Church Windows *(No Bake Cookie)*

12 oz. chocolate chips
1 stick oleo (1/2 c.)
1 (10-1/2 oz.) pkg. miniature colored marshmallows

1 c. walnuts (chopped)
1 (7 oz.) pkg. coconut

Melt chocolate chips and butter. Cool and add nuts and marshmallows. Divide mixture in half to form 2 large rolls. Roll each in coconut. Wrap in wax paper and chill for 24 hours. Slice into 1/3 inch cookies. Makes around 3 dozen cookies.

Butterscotch Squares

1 lb. brown sugar
1 c. butter
2 eggs
2 c. flour

1 t. baking powder
1/2 t. salt
1 c. walnuts (coarsely cut)

Cook sugar and butter in top of double boiler over hot water until sugar dissolves. Cool; add eggs, 1 at a time, beating well. Stir in other ingredients. Spread in ungreased jelly roll pan, 15 x 11 inches. Bake at 350° for 25 minutes. While hot, cut into 40 squares. Cut them small; they're rich.

Lemon Squares

2 c. flour
1/2 c. powdered sugar
1 c. butter
4 eggs (slightly beaten)

2 c. sugar
6 T. lemon juice
4 T. flour
1/2 t. baking powder

Mix 2 c. flour, powdered sugar, and butter together and pat in greased 9 x 13 inch pan. Bake 20-25 minutes at 350°. Mix beaten eggs, sugar, lemon juice, 4 T. flour and baking powder. Spread over top of first mixture and bake 20-25 minutes more. Sprinkle powdered sugar on top. Cut in squares and serve.

Lemon Squares

1 c. flour
1 stick oleo
1/4 c. confectioners' sugar
2 eggs

1 c. white sugar
1/2 t. baking powder
2-1/2 T. lemon juice (bottled, if desired)
Dash of salt

Sift flour and sugar into bowl. Blend in oleo with clean finger tips until well mixed. Pat evenly, with moistened fingers, into the bottom of an 8 x 8 inch baking pan which has been greased and floured. Bake for 15 minutes at 350°. Meanwhile beat together the eggs, sugar, baking powder, lemon juice and salt. Pour this mixture over the baked crust and return to oven for another 20 minutes, at same temperature. Cool. Cut in squares and sprinkle with confectioners' sugar.

This recipe can easily be doubled, but bake in a 9 x 13 inch pan. Bake for the same length of time.

Filled Date Bars

3/4 c. soft shortening (part butter)
1 c. brown sugar (packed)
1-3/4 c. flour

1/2 t. soda
1 t. salt
1-1/2 c. quick cooking rolled oats

DATE FILLING

3 c. dates (cut up)
1/4 c. sugar

1-1/2 c. water

Cook dates, sugar, and water over low heat, stirring constantly until thick, about 10 minutes. Cool.

Bars—Preheat oven to 400°. Mix shortening and sugar. Blend flour, soda, and salt; stir into sugar mixture. Mix in oats; flatten half of mixture into bottom of greased 13 x 9 x 2 inch pan. Spread with cooled date filling. Top with remaining crumb mixture, patting lightly. Bake 25-30 minutes. Cut into bars while warm.

Ritz Cracker Bars

4 egg whites

1 c. sugar

Beat into peaks and fold in 45 crushed Ritz crackers.

ADD:
1 t. vanilla

3/4 c. nuts (chopped)

Bake in lightly greased 9 x 13 inch pan, at 350° for 20-25 minutes.

FROST WITH:
1 small pkg. Cool Whip
1/4 c. powdered sugar

1 c. toasted coconut
1/2 t. vanilla

Chill 1 hour.

Sugar Cookies

1 c. sugar
1 c. butter
3 eggs
3 c. all-purpose flour

1 t. soda
2 t. cream of tartar
Ground lemon rind or
lemon extract

Mix in order given and refrigerate dough overnight. Roll out very thin on floured cloth. Bake at 400° on lightly greased cookie sheet until done.

7 Layer Bar

1/4 lb. butter
1 c. graham cracker crumbs
1 (6 oz.) pkg. chocolate chips
1 (6 oz.) pkg. peanut butter or
  butterscotch chips
1 c. coconut
1 c. nuts (chopped)
1 can Eagle Brand
  sweetened condensed milk

Melt butter in pan, sprinkle next ingredients in order given, covering with milk last. Bake 30 minutes at 350°. Cool before cutting.

M and M Cookies

1/2 c. Crisco
1/2 c. brown sugar
1/4 c. granulated sugar
1/2 t. vanilla
1/4 t. water
1 egg
1 c. plus 2 T. flour
1/2 t. salt
1/2 t. soda
3/4 c. M and M chocolate candies

Blend Crisco and sugars. Beat in vanilla, water and egg. Sift dry ingredients together and add to mixture. Mix well. Stir in M and Ms. Drop by t. on ungreased baking sheet. Bake 375° for 10 to 12 minutes.

Raisin or Fruit Cookies *(Soft)*

1 c. sugar
3/4 c. shortening
2 eggs
4 T. raisin liquid
1 c. raisins
1 t. cinnamon
1/2 t. salt
2-1/2 c. flour
1 t. soda

Boil raisins in 1 c. water for 20 minutes. Reserve 4 T. of the liquid and add the soda to it. Combine sugar, shortening, eggs; mix and add the dry ingredients alternately with the raisin liquid. For variation, nuts, fruit and raisins or gumdrops may be added. Drop by spoon on greased cookie sheet. Bake 325°.

Better is a dinner of herbs where love is than a
fatted ox and hatred with it.

Proverbs 14:17

Ella's White Sugar Cookies

1 c. butter
1 c. powdered sugar
1 egg
1-1/2 t. almond extract

1 t. vanilla
2-1/2 c. all-purpose flour (sift)
1 t. salt

Cream butter, add sugar gradually. Cream well. Add egg, almond and vanilla extracts. Sift flour and salt together, add to first mixture and blend. Roll 1/8 inch thick (very gently), cut with 3 inch cutters, sprinkle with colored sugars (or frost after baking). Place on greased cookie sheets, bake at 375° for 8 to 10 minutes. Makes 5 dozen cookies.

Miniature Caramel Apple Cookies

1/2 c. butter
1/4 c. brown sugar
1/4 c. powdered sugar
1/4 t. salt
1 egg
1 t. vanilla

2 c. flour
toothpicks
1/2 lb. or 36 caramels
1/2 lb. walnuts (chopped)
2/3 c. milk

Cream sugars and butter. Add salt, egg, vanilla, and flour. Shape dough into 1 inch balls. Bake 15 to 18 minutes, at 350°. Remove from oven, insert toothpicks. Melt caramels with milk in a double boiler. Dip in cookies to coat with caramel. Roll in nuts. Set on wax paper.

Note: Start to melt caramels before you mix cookies. It takes a long time to melt.

Pumpkin Cookies

1 c. white sugar
1 egg
1 t. vanilla
2 t. baking powder
2-1/2 c. flour

1 c. shortening
1 c. pumpkin
1 t. baking soda
1/2 t. salt

Cream sugar and shortening well. Beat in egg, pumpkin and vanilla. Sift dry ingredients and add to creamed mixture and mix thoroughly. Drop by t. on baking sheet. Bake 350° for 10 minutes. May frost and decorate if you like. Yield: 3 dozen.

Peanut Whirls

1/2 c. shortening
1 c. sugar
1 t. vanilla
1/2 t. salt
2 T. milk

1/2 c. chunk style peanut butter
1 egg
1-1/4 c. flour
1/2 t. soda
1 pkg. chocolate chips

Cream shortening, peanut butter, sugar, egg and vanilla. Spoon flour (not sifted) into dry measuring cup. Level off and pour measured flour onto a square of wax paper. Add salt and soda to flour (not sifted) and stir to blend. Add blended dry ingredients alternately with milk. Blend well.

Roll out cookie dough on a floured cloth or covered board to a rectangle 1/4 inch in thickness. Melt chocolate chips over hot water and cool slightly. Spread on rolled cookie dough. Roll up lengthwise, jelly roll fashion and chill for 1/2 hour. (Do not chill over 1/2 hour.) Slice with a sharp knife 1/8 inch thick and place on ungreased baking sheet. Bake at 350° for 8 to 10 minutes. Yield: 5-6 dozen cookies.

Carrot Cookies

1 c. shortening
3/4 c. sugar
1 c. carrots (mashed, cooked)
2 eggs
1 t. vanilla

2 c. flour
2 t. baking powder
1/2 t. salt
3/4 c. coconut

Combine ingredients in order given; drop by t. onto greased baking sheet. Bake in 400° oven for 8 to 10 minutes. Yield: 4-5 dozen.

Peanut Butter Cookies

1 c. shortening
1 c. peanut butter
2 c. brown sugar
2 eggs

2-1/2 c. all-purpose flour (sift)
1 t. soda
1 t. salt
1 t. baking powder

Cream shortening, peanut butter and brown sugar thoroughly. Add eggs and beat well. Add sifted dry ingredients. Form into tiny balls and place on greased cookie sheet. Press down with fork. Bake at 375° for 10 to 12 minutes. Yield: 6 dozen cookies.

Peanut Butter Cookies

1/2 c. shortening	3/4 t. soda
1/2 c. peanut butter	1/4 t. salt
1/2 c. white sugar	1/2 t. baking powder
1/2 c. brown sugar	1-1/4 c. flour
1 egg	

Cream shortening and peanut butter. Add sugars and egg. Add sifted dry ingredients. Cover and chill. Shape into small balls. Place on lightly greased baking sheet. Flatten with a fork dipped in water. Bake at 350° for about 15 minutes. Yields 3 dozen medium sized cookies.

Chocolate Pinwheel Cookies

2 c. chocolate chips	1 t. vanilla
2 T. butter	1/2 c. butter
2/3 c. Borden's sweetened condensed milk	1 c. brown sugar
2 t. vanilla	2 egg yolks
2 c. nuts (chopped)	2 c. flour
1/2 t. baking powder	

Melt chocolate chips and 2 T. butter in milk. Stir well, then add vanilla and nuts. Set aside to be used as filling.

Cream 1/2 c. butter, brown sugar, egg yolks and vanilla. Add flour and baking powder. Roll this dough out to about 24 x 9 inch rectangle. Spread chocolate filling over it. Roll up. Chill in refrigerator until firm. Slice in 1/2 inch slices. Bake on aluminum foil for 10 minutes, in 350° oven.

Mom's Brown Sugar Cookies

2 c. brown sugar	1 t. salt
2 eggs	1 t. soda
1 c. lard (or vegetable shortening)	1 t. cream of tartar
3 c. flour (not sifted)	1 t. vanilla
granulated sugar	

Cream sugar, eggs, vanilla and lard. Add flour, salt, soda and cream of tartar. Form into balls the size of a walnut. Dip top in granulated sugar. Place on ungreased tins. Bake at 350° for 8-10 minutes.

Fruit Punch Bars

2 eggs	1-1/2 t. soda
1-1/2 c. sugar	1/2 t. salt
1 lb. 1 oz. can fruit cocktail	1 t. vanilla
(undrained)	1-1/3 c. flaked coconut
2-1/4 c. flour	1/2 c. nuts

Grease, flour bottom of 15 x 10 x 1 inch jelly roll pan. Beat eggs and sugar in large bowl at high speed until light and fluffy. Add fruit cocktail, flour, soda, salt and vanilla. Beat at medium speed until well blended, scraping sides and bottom of bowl. Spread in pan. Sprinkle with coconut and nuts. Bake at 350° for 20 to 25 minutes or until golden brown. While hot, drizzle with glaze. Cool and cut into bars or serving pieces.

GLAZE

3/4 c. sugar	1/2 t. vanilla
1/2 c. butter	1/2 c. nuts
1/4 c. evaporated milk	

Combine all ingredients except nuts in small pan. Bring to boiling; boil 2 minutes stirring constantly. Remove from heat; stir in nut and cool. Spread over pastry.

Note: Make this up while bars are baking, or before baking, to allow time to cool.

Oatmeal Cookies

1/2 c. margarine	1 t. baking soda
1/2 c. vegetable oil	2 T. wheat germ
1-1/4 c. brown sugar	1/2 t. cinnamon
2 eggs	1-1/2 c. whole wheat flour
1 t. vanilla	3 c. rolled oats
1 t. salt	1/2 c. raisins (chopped)
3 T. milk	

Mix margarine, oil and brown sugar well. Add eggs, one at a time, mix well. Add vanilla, salt, and milk. Add dry ingredients. Add oats and raisins. Bake on greased cookie sheets in 350° oven for 10-15 minutes.

Oatmeal Cookies

1 c. sugar
1/2 c. shortening
2 eggs
1 c. raisins
5 T. liquid from stewed raisins

1 t. baking soda
2 c. oatmeal
2 c. flour
1/2 c. nuts

Stew raisins in small amount of water for about 5 minutes. Drain; reserving 5 T. liquid. Cream sugar and shortening; add eggs, mixing well. Add oatmeal and flour alternately with raisin liquid mixed with soda. Fold in raisins and nuts. Use greased cookie sheet, drop cookies with t. Bake at 375° for 10 to 12 minutes.

Ranger Cookies

1 c. shortening
1 c. white sugar
1 c. brown sugar
2 eggs
1 t. vanilla
2 c. flour

1/2 t. salt
1 t. soda
1/2 t. baking powder
2 c. quick oats
2 c. Rice Krispies
1 c. shredded coconut

Cream together shortening, sugars, eggs and vanilla. Sift together flour, salt, soda, and baking powder. Add to creamed mixture. Stir in oats, Krispies and coconut. Bake at 350°.

Sugar Cookies

1 c. sugar
1c. butter
3 eggs
3 c. all-purpose flour

1 t. soda
2 t. cream of tartar
ground lemon rind or lemon extract

Mix in order given and refrigerate dough overnight. Roll out very thin on flour cloth. Bake at 400° on lightly greased cookie sheet until done.

Housework is something you do that nobody
notices unless you don't do it.

Apple Bars

2-1/2 c. flour
1 t. salt
1 c. shortening
1 egg yolk
1 c. corn flakes

8 to 10 tart apples (sliced 8 c.)
3/4 to 1 c. sugar
1 t. cinnamon
1 egg white
1 c. powdered sugar and 3-4 T. milk

Combine flour and salt. Cut in shortening. Beat egg yolk and add enough milk to make 2/3 cup. Stir into flour mixture. Roll half of dough 17 x 12 inches to fit into and up sides of 15 1/2 x 10 1/2 x 1 inch pan. Sprinkle corn flakes on dough, top with apples. Combine sugar and cinnamon, sprinkle on apples. Roll rest of dough and place over apples. Seal edges. Cut slits in top crust. Beat egg white only until frothy and brush on crust. Bake 375° for 50 minutes. Combine 1 c. powdered sugar, 3 to 4 T. milk and drizzle on warm bars.

Cookie Sheet Brownie Cake with Icing

2 c. flour
2 c. sugar
1 stick oleo (1/2 c.)
1/2 c. shortening or oil
3 T. cocoa

1 c. water
2 eggs
1/2 c. buttermilk
1 t. baking soda

ICING

1 stick oleo (1/2 c.)
3 T. cocoa
1 box confectioners' sugar (2 c.)

6 T. cream or condensed milk
1 t. vanilla
1/2 c. nuts

Grease and flour cookie sheet. Set oven for 325°. Mix flour and sugar and make well in middle. Put oleo, oil, cocoa, and water in saucepan. Bring to a boil and remove from stove. Add to flour and sugar mixture. Add eggs, beaten slightly. Put buttermilk in 2 c. container and stir in baking soda. Add this to cake batter. Mix well, no beating necessary. Bake for 25 minutes.

After cake has cooled 5 minutes, put on icing: melt oleo and cocoa. Remove from stove and add confectioners' sugar, cream, vanilla and nuts.

Mounds Bars

1 stick oleo	7 oz. or 2-2/3 c. coconut
2 c. graham cracker crumbs	1/2 c. nuts
1 can Eagle Brand sweetened condensed milk	2 small pkg. chocolate chips

Mix oleo and crumbs, put in 9 x 11 inch pan, bake at 350° for 10 minutes. Mix milk, coconut, and nuts; spread on baked crumbs and bake again for 15 minutes. Melt chocolate chips and spread on baked bars. Allow to cool several hours until chocolate is set.

Orange Date Bars

3/4 c. oleo or half shortening & oleo	1/2 t. salt
3/4 c. brown sugar	1 t. soda
2 eggs	1 t. hot water
1 t. vanilla	1 t. hot milk
1-1/2 c. flour	

FILLING

1/2 c. chopped dates	10 orange candy slices (cut up)
1/2 c. sugar	3/4 c. water
2 T. flour	1/2 c. nuts

Cream together shortening, sugar, eggs and vanilla; add dry ingredients alternately with hot water and hot milk. Boil the filling until thick. Cool and add 1/2 c. nuts; spread 1/2 of first mixture in bottom of pan. Spread with filling. Cover with remaining topping. Bake 25 minutes or more at 350°.

Pineapple Bars

1 pkg. yellow cake mix	3 T. oleo (melted)
3 egg yolks	

Mix and pat in 9 x 13 inch pan. Beat 3 egg whites stiff. Add:

1/2 c. white sugar	1 c. coconut
1 c. crushed pineapple (drain)	

Place egg white mixture over top crust. Sprinkle with nuts. Bake at 350° for 30 minutes.

Tri-Level Brownies

FIRST LAYER

1/2 c. flour (sifted)
1/4 t. baking soda
1/4 t. salt

1 c. quick cooking rolled oats
1/2 c. brown sugar
6 T. butter or oleo (melted)

SECOND LAYER

1 square (1 oz.) unsweetened
   chocolate (melted)
4 T. butter or oleo (melted)
3/4 c. granulated sugar
1 egg
2/3 c. flour (sifted)

1/4 t. baking powder
1/4 t. salt
1/4 c. milk
1/2 t. vanilla
1/2 c. walnuts (chopped)

First layer—For bottom layer, sift together flour, soda, and salt; mix with rolled oats and the brown sugar. Stir in butter. Pat mixture into 11 x 7 x 1-1/2 inch pan. Bake at 350° for 10 minutes.

Second layer—For middle layer, combine chocolate, melted butter and sugar; add egg and beat well. Sift together flour, baking powder, and salt; add alternately with milk and vanilla to chocolate mixture. Fold in nuts. Spread batter over baked layer. Return to oven and bake at 350° for 25 minutes more.

TOP LAYER

1 square (1 oz.) unsweetened chocolate
2 T. butter or oleo

1-1/2 c. confectioners' sugar
1 t. vanilla

Place chocolate and butter in small saucepan. Stir over low heat until chocolate melts. Remove from heat and add confectioners' sugar and vanilla. Blend in enough water (about 2 T.) to make almost pourable consistency. Spread over baked brownies. To serve, cut in bars. Top each with a walnut half (optional). Makes 16 large bars.

Rainbow Marshmallow Cookies

1 stick oleo
1 (12 oz.) pkg. chocolate chips
3 eggs

2 or more c. powdered sugar
1 pkg. colored marshmallows
coconut

Melt oleo and chocolate chips. Add eggs and cook 2 minutes. Cool. Add marshmallows. Knead into rolls on coconut.

Chocolate Chip Cookies

2/3 c. shortening (part butter
   or margarine)
1/2 c. granulated sugar
1/2 c. brown sugar (packed)
1 egg
1 t. vanilla

1-1/2 c. flour
1/2 t. soda
1/2 t. salt
1/2 c. nuts (chopped)
1 pkg. (6 oz.) semi-sweet
   chocolate pieces (1 c.)

Heat oven to 375° (quick moderate). Mix shortening, sugars, egg, and vanilla thoroughly. Measure flour by sifting. (For a softer cookie, add 1/4 c. more flour.) Stir dry ingredients together; blend in shortening mixture. Add nuts and chocolate pieces. Drop rounded t. of dough about 2 inches apart on ungreased baking sheet.

Bake 8 to 10 minutes or until delicately browned. (Cookies should still be soft). Cool slightly before removing from baking sheet. Makes 4 to 5 dozen 2 inch cookies. Note: if you use Gold Medal flour (self-rising), omit soda and salt.

Oatmeal Squares

1 c. brown sugar
3/4 c. shortening
2 eggs (well beaten)
1/2 c. sour milk
1/2 t. vanilla
2 c. oatmeal

2 c. flour
1 c. raisins or dates (chopped)
1 t. soda
1 t. cinnamon
1 t. salt

Cream shortening; add sugar. Add eggs and vanilla. Mix well and add oatmeal. Mix and sift flour, salt and cinnamon and combine with fruit. Dissolve soda in milk. Add to first mixture, mix well. Add remaining dry ingredients. Mix until smooth. Spread in greased pan. Bake in moderate oven, 350°, until done. Cool and cut in squares.

Nut Fudge Brownies

1/2 c.oleo
1 c. sugar
2 eggs
4 T. cocoa

3 T. boiling water
1 c. flour (sifted)
1 t. vanilla
1/2 c. nuts

Mix with electric beater oleo, sugar, and eggs. Add cocoa mixed to paste with boiling water. Then add flour, vanilla, and nuts. Bake in 350° oven, frost with fudge frosting.

Apple Dream Bars

PIE CRUST MIXTURE

2 c. flour

12 T. oleo or margarine

1/2 c. sugar

Pat into a 9 x 13 cake pan. Bake at 350° for 20 minutes.

FILLING

2 eggs (beaten)

1 c. brown sugar

1 t. vanilla

1/2 c. flour

1 t. baking powder

pinch of salt

1/4 c. nuts

2 c. diced apples

Spread apple mixture on baked crust and bake 35 minutes more.

Chocolate Cookie Squares

1 t. soda

1 c. boiling water

2 c. dates (cut up)

2 eggs

1 c. shortening (part butter)

1 c. sugar

1-3/4 c. flour (sifted)

2 T. cocoa

1/2 t. salt

1 c. chocolate chips

1 c. nuts (chopped)

1 t. vanilla

Chocolate Frosting

Dissolve soda in water; pour over dates and let cool. Beat eggs and shortening and sugar until fluffy. Sift flour, cocoa, and salt together. Add alternately with date mixture to egg mixture. Stir in remaining ingredients. Spread in greased and floured 18 x 10 x 1 inch pan. Bake at 350° for 25 to 30 minutes.

CHOCOLATE FROSTING

1-1/2 c. sugar

3 T. cocoa

1/2 c. milk

2 T. butter

Mix sugar, cocoa, milk and butter; boil 3 minutes. Cool. Beat until thick; spread on cooled cookie squares. Yield: 4 dozen

Mealtime: When youngsters sit down and
continue to eat.

Apricot Almond Bars

1 c. butter
1/2 c. sugar
1/2 t. vanilla
2 c. flour
1 (12 oz.) jar apricot jam

2 egg whites
1/2 t. almond extract
1/4 c. slivered almonds
1 c. powdered sugar

Cream butter, sugar, and vanilla until light and fluffy. Add flour. Mix thoroughly. Put into 9 x 13 inch pan, bake at 350° for 15 minutes. Cool. Spread jam over crust. Beat egg whites and powdered sugar; add almond extract. Mixture acts as a glaze as is thin. Spread carefully over jam. Top with almonds. Bake at 400° for 20 minutes.

Pumpkin Bars

1 c. Crisco
1 c. sugar
1 c. pumpkin
1 egg
1 t. vanilla
pinch of salt

2 c. flour
1 t. baking powder
1 t. baking soda
1 (6 oz.) pkg. chocolate chips
nuts (optional)
raisins (optional)

Mix first 5 ingredients together. Add dry ingredients and mix. Add chocolate chips, nuts and raisins if desired. Bake at 350° for 25 minutes. Glaze with mixture of powdered sugar, orange or lemon juice and melted butter.

Special K Bars

1 c. sugar
1 c. Karo white syrup
6 c. Special K cereal

1 c. peanut butter
1/2 small pkg. chocolate chips
1 small pkg. butterscotch chips

Heat sugar and syrup just to boiling point (when bubbles start to form). Don't boil. Remove from heat. Add peanut butter. Pour over Special K in a large bowl. Mix well. Press into greased 9 x 13 inch pan. Melt chips and use to frost bars after cooled. Cut into small bars after frosting has set. (It may help to cool them in refrigerator so frosting sets more quickly.)

Fudge Nut Bars

12 oz. pkg. chocolate chips	2 eggs
1 can Bordens sweetened	2 c. brown sugar
condensed milk	2 t. vanilla
2 T. oleo	2-1/2 c. flour
1/2 t. salt	1 t. soda
1/2 c. nutmeats (if desired)	1 t. salt
2 t. vanilla	3 c. oatmeal
1 stick oleo and 1/2 c. Crisco	

Melt together the chocolate chips, Borden's milk, 2 T. oleo and 1/2 t. salt. Add the nuts and 2 t. vanilla. Set this aside while you cream together the oleo and shortening, eggs, brown sugar, and 2 t. vanilla. Add the flour, soda, salt, and oatmeal to the shortening mixture. Pat 2/3 of this mixture into 9 x 13 inch greased cake pan. Pour the chocolate mixture over this. Crumble the remaining 1/3 mixture on top. Bake 30 minutes at 350°.

Toffee Bars

1/2 c. butter	1 c. brown sugar
1/2 c. shortening	

Mix ingredients together and add:

1 egg yolk (beaten)	2 c. flour
1 t. vanilla	1/2 t. salt

Mix. Pat batter on cookie sheet. Bake 15 minutes in 350° oven. Melt 1/2 lb. Hershey bar over hot water (not boiling). Spread over baked mixture. Top with grated walnuts. Cut in squares.

There is one thing sure, my unknown friend
On which good cooking will depend.
Remember this, when you commence
To use a little Common Sense.

Pies and Pastries

Apple Crumble Pie

apples (sliced)
1 stick oleo
granulated white sugar
water (if necessary)

1 c. flour
1 c. brown sugar
cinnamon

Fill baking dish with sliced apples. Sprinkle with white sugar according to tartness of apples. Sprinkle with cinnamon. Add small amount of water according to juiciness of apples, some varieties may need no water. Make topping by mixing together the flour, brown sugar, and melted oleo. Pat topping down lightly on apples and bake at 350° until apples are done.

Apple Pie Variations

FRENCH APPLE PIE

Instead of top crust use crumb topping over apple slices as follows: mix until crumbly 1/2 c. butter, 1/2 c. brown sugar firmly packed, and 1 c. sifted flour. Bake as usual, serve warm with whipped cream or ice cream.

DUTCH APPLE PIE

Make apple pie as usual with top crust, except make extra large slits in top crust. About 5 minutes before pie is done remove pie from oven, pour 1/2 c. heavy cream through slits in top crust. Return to oven and bake 5 minutes more.

*When God measures man, He puts the tape
around the heart, not the head.*

Ready Mix Pie Crust

3 lb. can shortening (Fluffo)
handful of salt
18 c. flour

Mix well with pastry blender in large bowl. Store dry mix in covered cans on shelf (or refrigerator if keeping for a longer time.) When ready to roll pie crust use 2 c. dry mix with 1/4 c. water—for a double crust.

Paper-Bag Apple Pie

1 unbaked 9 inch pie shell
about 2-1/2 lb. apples
1/2 c. sugar (for filling)
2 T. flour (for filling)
1/2 t. cinnamon
2 T. lemon juice
1/2 c. sugar (for topping)
1/2 c. flour (for topping)
1/2 c. oleo or butter

Pare, core, and quarter apples, halve each quarter crosswise to make chunks. Place in large bowl.

Combine 1/2 c. sugar, 2 T. flour, cinnamon in cup. Sprinkle over apples, toss, spoon into pie shell and drizzle with lemon juice. Combine 1/2 c. sugar, 1/2 c. flour, cut in butter. Sprinkle over apples to cover. Slide pie into a brown paper bag, large enough to cover pie loosely; fold open end over twice and fasten with paper clips. Place on large cookie sheet for easy handling.

Bake at 425° for 1 hour or more (depending on apples). Pie will be done when top is golden and bubbly. Split bag open and remove pie to cool.

Pumpkin Pie *(Spicy)*

1-3/4 c. mashed pumpkin
1/2 t. salt
1-3/4 c. milk
3 eggs or 4 yolks
2/3 c. brown sugar (packed)
1 (9 inch) unbaked pie crust
2 T. granulated sugar
1-1/4 t. cinnamon
1/2 t. ginger
1/2 t. nutmeg
1/4 t. cloves

Beat all ingredients together with rotary beater. Pour into unbaked pie shell, bake in 400° or 425° oven for 45 to 55 minutes. Test with silver knife, done if it comes out clean. The center may look slightly soft but will set as it cools. Serve slightly warm or cold.

Blue Ribbon Pumpkin Pie

2 eggs
1 c. canned pumpkin
3/4 c. sugar
1/3 t. cinnamon
Unbaked pie shell

1/3 t. ginger
1/3 t. vanilla
1/4 t. salt
1-1/2 c. milk or half and half

Combine all ingredients, beat with rotary beater, pour into unbaked pie shell. Bake very slowly.

Magic Pumpkin Pie

1 (unbaked 9 inch) pastry shell
2 c. canned pumpkin
1-1/3 c. sweetened condensed milk
1 egg

1/2 t. salt
1/2 t. nutmeg
1/2 t. ginger
1/2 t. cinnamon

In large mixing bowl blend all ingredients. Pour into pie shell. Bake in 375° moderate oven until sharp blade knife inserted near center comes out clean, 50-55 minutes. Cool.

Streusel Cream Peach Pie

4 c. peaches (fresh, sliced, peeled)
1/2 c. sugar
1/2 t. nutmeg

1 egg
2 T. cream
1 unbaked pie shell (9 inch)

TOPPING
1/4 c. brown sugar
1/4 c. soft butter

1/2 c. flour

Sprinkle sugar and nutmeg over sliced peaches in unbaked pie crust. Beat egg and cream and pour over peaches and sugar. Mix topping ingredients until crumbly and sprinkle over peaches. Bake at 400° for 35 to 45 minutes. Serve slightly warm. Very nice to garnish with whipped cream or cultured sour cream.

Rhubarb Meringue Pie

Make your usual crust for one pie shell (unbaked)

FILLING
2 c. rhubarb
2 egg yolks
1 c. sugar
2 T. flour
1/2 t. salt

MERINGUE
2 egg whites
1/4 t. baking powder
4 T. sugar

Filling: Wash and dice rhubarb. Pour boiling water over and drain. Beat egg yolks, add sugar, flour and salt. Beat and pour mixture over rhubarb. Stir and mix well. Pour into lined pie tin and bake at 350° for 45 minutes. Cool and cover with meringue.

Meringue: Beat egg whites until frothy. Add baking powder and beat until stiff. Add sugar and beat again. Put on pie; put in oven and bake 15 minutes at 300°.

Heikki Lunta Pie

1 baked pie shell
1/3 c. sugar
3 T. flour
1 pkg. gelatin (Knox)
1/4 t. salt
1-1/3 c. milk

1/2 t. vanilla
1/2 t. almond flavoring
2 egg whites
1/4 t. cream of tartar
1/3 c. sugar
1/3 to 1/2 c. whipping cream

Mix first 4 ingredients in saucepan, add milk gradually. Cook over medium heat until boiling, boil 1 minute, stirring. Put saucepan in cold water. Cool until other ingredients are mixed. Add vanilla and almond extract. Beat egg whites with cream of tartar and sugar. Now beat cream. Fold all three together and spoon into baked pie shell. If desired, beat remaining cream for top of pie.

Heikki Lunta was a legendary character of the hermit type who lived in a shack off the back-roads of the Northern mid-west. A song was composed about him which was rather popular one winter. Whenever Heikki Lunta danced it would snow, the faster he danced the harder it snowed!

Raspberry Pie

1 qt. raspberries
1 c. water
1 c. sugar
1-1/2 t. cornstarch

1 T. raspberry Kool-Aid
1 T. gelatin
1/4 c. cold water
graham cracker crust

Wash berries and drain. Cook water, sugar, cornstarch and Kool-Aid until clear. Add gelatin which has been dissolved in 1/4 c. cold water. Cool. When mixture congeals, add berries and pour into graham cracker crust. Put to set in refrigerator. Serve with whipped cream or topping mix.

Strawberry Pie

1 baked 9 inch pie shell
1 qt. fresh strawberries

2 T. cornstarch
1 c. sugar

Boil 1 pt. strawberries with 2 T. cornstarch and 1 c. sugar, until it coats on spoon. Put 1 pt. of berries in baked pie shell. Pour cooled, boiled mixture on top and refrigerate until ready to serve. Top with whipped cream or topping mix.

Rhubarb Pie *(Custard)*

4 c. rhubarb (diced)
1/4 c. orange juice
2 T. butter
2 whole eggs
unbaked pie shell

1-1/2 c. sugar
3 T. flour
1/4 t. salt
1/4 t. nutmeg

Beat eggs and mix all ingredients together. Pour into unbaked pie shell, top with pastry cut-outs or lattice top. Bake at 450° for 15 minutes, reduce heat, bake at 350° for 35 minutes longer.

Rhubarb Pie

3 T. flour
1 c. sugar
Pastry for double crust

2 c. rhubarb
1 egg (well beaten)

Sift flour with sugar. Add egg, well beaten. Mix together and add rhubarb. Double crust. Bake in hot oven 450° for 10 minutes, reduce heat to 350° for 30 minutes.

Hawaiian Lime Pie

1 pkg. Jello lime pudding mix
1/3 c. sugar
Dash of salt
1/4 c. water
2 eggs (separated)

1 c. water
1 c. pineapple juice
1 baked pie shell or graham
   cracker crust (9 inch)
Whipped cream or Dream Whip

Combine pie filling, 1/3 c. sugar, salt and water in saucepan. Mix in egg yolks, 1 c. water, and pineapple juice. Cook and stir over medium heat until mixture comes to a full boil, about 5 minutes. Beat egg whites foamy, add sugar, beating until soft peaks form, fold into hot pudding. Pour into pie shell. Garnish with whipped cream or Dream Whip and pineapple chunks.

Quick Christmas Pie

1 can (18 oz.) ready-to-serve
   vanilla pudding
1/2 t. almond extract
1 envelope (about 2 oz.)
   dessert topping mix

1-3/4 c. shredded coconut (divided)
1 (9 inch) baked pie shell
1/3 c. water
About 4 drops green food coloring
Red maraschino cherries (halved)

In bowl, blend pudding and extract. Prepare topping mix as direct on package. Fold topping into pudding mixture; fold in 1 c. of the coconut. Pour mixture into pie shell.

In small bowl, combine water and food coloring. Stir in remaining coconut; drain on paper toweling and allow to dry about 10 minutes. Sprinkle tinted coconut around edge of pie in wreath shape, garnish with cherries. Chill at least 2 hours or until set.

Bittersweet Pie

1 c. milk
1/4 t. salt
1/2 c. shaved
   unsweetened chocolate

20 marshmallows
1/2 t. almond flavoring
1 c. heavy cream (whipped)
1 baked 9 inch pastry shell

Heat marshmallows and milk, stir until marshmallows dissolve. Add salt and flavoring; chill. Fold in whipped cream and shaved chocolate, reserving a little for top garnish. Turn into cooled shell, garnish with chocolate and chill several hours.

White Christmas Pie

1 baked pastry shell
  (high edges)
1 T. unflavored gelatin
1/4 c. cold water
1/2 c. sugar
4 T. flour
1/2 t. salt
1-1/2 c. milk

3/4 t. vanilla
1/4 t. almond extract
1/2 c. whipping cream
3 egg whites
1/4 t. cream of tartar
1/2 c. sugar
1 c. moist shredded coconut
1 pkg. frozen strawberries (thaw)

Soften gelatin in water. Mix sugar, flour, and salt in small saucepan. Gradually add milk. Cook over low heat stirring until it boils. Boil 1 minute. Remove from heat and stir in softened gelatin. Cool. When partially set, beat with beater until smooth. Blend in vanilla and almond extract. In another bowl whipping cream. Add to mixture. Make a meringue of egg whites, cream of tartar and sugar. Fold into whip cream-pudding mixture. Add most of the coconut (save some for garnishing). Fill the cooled pastry shell. Garnish with coconut. Refrigerate for at least 2 hours. When serving pie, top with frozen strawberries (thawed).

Sunny Silver Pie

1/2 T. Knox gelatin
4 T. cold water
4 egg whites
1/2 c. sugar

4 egg yolks
1/2 c. sugar
3 T. lemon juice

Soak gelatin in cold water until thoroughly set. Beat egg yolks and 1/2 c. sugar together well. Add lemon juice. Cook over hot water until thick. Beat in gelatin. Whip egg whites until stiff and add 1/2 c. sugar. Add cooked mixture, heating well. Pour into baked pie shell and chill. Serve with whipped cream.

NOTE
1 recipe fills good sized pie shell
1-1/2 recipes fills 2 pie shells
2 recipes fills 3 pie shells

He who can take advice is sometimes superior to
him who can give it.

Oatmeal Pie

1/4 c. butter
1/2 c. sugar
1/2 t. cinnamon
1/2 t. ground cloves
1/4 t. salt

1 c. dark corn syrup
3 eggs
1 c. quick cook oatmeal
1 unbaked pie shell

Cream together butter and sugar. Add cinnamon, cloves, and salt. Stir in syrup. Add eggs, 1 at a time, stirring well. Stir in rolled oats. Pour into unbaked pie shell. Bake in moderate oven 350° for about 1 hour or until knife comes out clean. During baking the oatmeal forms chewy, "nutty" top crust. Pie is rich, delicately spiced.

French Cream Pie

1/2 c. heavy cream
1 4-oz. pkg. vanilla instant pudding
Sweetened fresh strawberries

1-1/3 c. milk
1 baked 9 inch graham cracker crust

Whip cream just until soft peaks form. Prepare pie filling using the 1-1/3 c. milk. Cool slightly. Fold in whipped cream. Pour into baked crust. Chill at least 1 hour. Cut into individual portions, spoon sweetened strawberries over each serving, if desired.

Pet Milk Date Pie

1 unbaked pie shell
1/4 c. butter
3/4 c. sugar
1/8 t. salt

2 eggs
1 c. evaporated milk
1 c. pitted dates
vanilla

Cream together until light and fluffy: butter, sugar and salt. Add eggs, slightly beaten. Add milk and vanilla, stir in dates (cut in small pieces). Pour into unbaked crust, bake in 450° oven for 10 minutes, reduce temperature to 350° for 40 minutes.

Oleo Pie Crust

1 stick oleo
1 c. flour

1/2 t. salt
4 T. water

Makes enough crust for 1 double 9 inch pie or 2 single pie shells.

Perfect Pie Crust

4 c. unsifted all-purpose flour
  (not instant or self-rising;
  lightly spooned into cup)
1 T. sugar
2 t. salt

1-3/4 c. solid vegetable
  shortening (not refrigerated;
  do not use oil, lard, or butter)
1 T. white or cider vinegar
1/2 c. water
1 large egg

Put first 3 ingredients in large bowl and mix well with table fork. Add shortening and mix with fork until ingredients are crumbly. In small bowl, beat together with fork 1/2 c. water, the vinegar, and egg. Combine the 2 mixtures, stirring with fork until all ingredients are moistened. Divide dough in 5 portions and, with hands, shape each portion in a flat round patty reading for rolling. Wrap each in plastic or wax paper and chill at least 1/2 hour.

Blueberry Pie

2 c. fresh blueberries
1 c. sugar
3 T. tapioca

1 t. lemon juice
10 large marshmallows (quartered)

Combine above ingredients and pour into an unbaked pie shell. Dot with 2 T. margarine. Top with strips of pastry, crisscross fashion. Trim edges. Bake at 450° for 10 minutes, reduce heat to 325° and bake 25 minutes longer.

Tiny English Currant Tarts

1 c. brown sugar
1 egg
3 t. butter
2 t. corn syrup

1 t. vanilla
1 c. dried currants
pastry for 9 inch crust
hot water

Pour hot water over currants to cover. Let stand while you prepare rest of filling. Mix sugar and butter together and add egg and syrup and vanilla. Squeeze water from currants and add. Mix well. Line 6 tart or muffin pans with pastry. Place 2 large spoonfuls of filling in each. Bake at 350° for 20-30 minutes, or until pastry is browned and filling is set.

Count Me As One

I like a neighbor who comes to borrow
A cup of sugar to "return tomorrow."
I like a neighbor who stops to talk
When I'm taking the baby out for a walk.
I like a neighbor to visit with me
Over cinnamon toast and a cup of tea.
A recipe shared has added flavor—
Count me as one who likes a neighbor.

Desserts and Tortes

Easy Date-Crumble Torte

Date Bar mix

walnuts (chopped)

frozen whipped topping

butter or margarine (melted)

Combine the crumb portion of 1 pkg. date bar mix and 1/2 c. chopped walnuts, stir in 2 T. butter, mix well. Spread in 9 x 13 inch pan, bake in hot oven 400° for 10 minutes. Break up with fork, cool and crumble. Prepare date filling according to directions. Cool. Place half of crumbs in bottom of 10 x 6 inch baking pan. Cover with 1/2 c. thawed topping, then with date mixture. Repeat with crumbs and whipped topping layers. Chill overnight. Top each serving with walnut half. Makes 8 squares.

Fruit Cocktail Torte

CRUST

20 graham crackers

1/2 c. margarine

1/2 c. sugar

Combine.

FRUIT COCKTAIL FILLING

1/2 c. milk

1/2 lb. marshmallows

1/2 pt. cream, whipped

1 large can fruit cocktail, drained

Heat milk and add marshmallows. Let set until marshmallows are melted. Cool. Add whipped cream and fruit cocktail.

Put crumb mixture in large cake pan, saving a little for sprinkling on top of filling. Pour in fruit cocktail mixture. Spread evenly and sprinkle with remaining crumbs. Let set in refrigerator.

Nabisco Torte

1 lb. Nabiscos (ground)
3/4 c. soft butter or oleo
1 c. powdered sugar
2 eggs (separated)

1/3 c. nuts (chopped)
1 qt. sweetened strawberries
1 c. cream (whipped)

Cream butter and sugar until fluffy. Add egg yolks and beat. Add beaten egg whites. Whip cream, fold in strawberries and nuts. Pack half of Nabisco crumbs in 9 x 13 inch pan. Spread butter mixture over top of crumbs. Spread fruit mixture over and top with rest of crumbs. Chill 24 hours. Serves 12.

Forgotten Torte

6 egg whites
1-1/2 c. sugar
1/2 t. salt
1/2 t. cream of tartar

1 t. vanilla
frozen raspberries
1/2 pt. whipping cream

Beat egg whites until foamy. Add salt, vanilla and cream of tartar and beat until it peaks. Add sugar 1 T. at a time until it is very stiff and holds up. Put into buttered pan 9 x 9 inches. Preheat oven to 450°. Turn off the oven when you put it in and leave in all night with oven off. Whip cream and spread over the top when you remove it from the oven. Put in refrigerator for about 5 hours. Put red raspberries (thawed) over the top when you serve it.

Blueberry Buckle

3/4 c. sugar
1/4 c. butter
1 egg
2 c. blueberries

1/2 c. milk
2 c. flour
2 t. baking powder
1/4 t. salt

Cream sugar, butter, and egg; blend in milk, flour, salt, and baking powder. Stir in drained blueberries. Spread batter in 7 x 13 inch pan. Sprinkle with the following:

2/3 c. sugar
1/4 c. flour

1/2 t. cinnamon
1/3 c. butter (melted)

Bake at 350° for 35 to 40 minutes.

Blueberry Buckle Dessert

BATTER

2 c. flour
2-1/2 t. baking powder
1/4 t. salt
1/2 c. butter

1/2 c. sugar
1 egg (well beaten)
1/2 c. milk

CRUMBLES

1/2 c. flour
1/2 t. cinnamon
2 c. fresh blueberries

1/4 c. butter
1/2 c. sugar

For batter, sift flour, baking powder and salt; and set aside. Cream butter and sugar, add egg. Mix well. Add dry ingredients alternately with milk. Pour into well greased oblong pan. Sprinkle blueberries over batter. Combine the crumble ingredients until crumbly and sprinkle over blueberries. Bake 350° for 45-50 minutes. Serve warm.

Elegant Cheese Squares

1 c. graham cracker crumbs
3 T. sugar
1/4 c. soft butter
1 pkg. (8 oz.) cream cheese
1/2 c. sugar
lemon slices, cherry halves for garnish

1/8 t. salt
1/2 c. milk
1 t. lemon juice
1 t. vanilla
1-1/2 c. Cool Whip (thawed)

Combine crumbs, sugar and soft butter, mix well. Press firmly into bottom and sides of 8 inch pan. Bake at 375° for 8 minutes. Cool. Beat cheese until fluffy, add sugar gradually, add salt; blend in milk, lemon juice and vanilla. Then blend in Cool Whip. Spoon into crumb-lined pan, chill until set, at least 3 hours. Cut into squares, garnish with lemon slices or cherry halves if desired.

Apricot Torte

1 lb. dried apricots
1 c. water
1 lb. marshmallows

1 c. cream (whipped)
1 crumb crust

Cut apricots fine and cook with water. Mash or strain. Add marshmallows and beat until dissolved. Cool. Add cream, whipped stiff. Pour into crumb crust.

Apple Torte
CRUST
Mix together with pie blender:

2 c. all-purpose flour
1/2 t. salt
3/4 c. brown sugar

3/4 c. shortening
2 c. quick cooking oatmeal

FILLING
6-7 c. apples

BEAT TOGETHER:

8 eggs (beaten)
3 c. sugar

1/2 c. all-purpose flour
dash of salt

Line a 10 x 14 inch cake pan with all but 1 cup of the oatmeal mixture, pressing it down firmly. Put apples into the crust. Pour the filling over the apples and sprinkle the remaining cup of oatmeal mixture over this. Lightly sprinkle the top of torte with cinnamon and dot with dabs of butter. Bake in 350° oven for about 1 hour or until custard is done when knife comes out clean.

Fruit Cocktail Torte

30 marshmallows
1/2 c. milk
1/2 c. whipping cream
1/2 t. vanilla

1 can fruit cocktail (drained)
1 can crushed pineapple (drained)
graham cracker crust

Melt marshmallows with milk. Stir constantly until all marshmallows are melted and fluffy. Whip cream until stiff. Add vanilla and fold into cooled marshmallows. Fold in 1 can of each (drained) fruit cocktail and pineapple. Pour into graham cracker crust.

GRAHAM CRACKER CRUST

1-1/2 c. graham cracker crumbs
1/4 c. butter (melted)

1/4 c. sugar

Roll graham crackers to make about 1-1/2 c. crumbs. Add sugar, melted butter, and mix thoroughly. Save about 2 T. to sprinkle on top of torte.

Pineapple Torte

1 lb. Nabiscos
1 c. pecans
1 c. powdered sugar
2/3 c. butter (melted)

2 eggs (slightly beaten)
1 t. vanilla
1 large can crushed pineapple
1 pt. heavy cream

Grind 1 lb. Nabiscos and set aside 3/4 c. of crumbs for topping. Line 8 x 10 inch pans with wax paper. Pack crumbs in bottom of pan. Over crumbs sprinkle chopped pecans. Cover with filling of powdered sugar, butter, eggs and vanilla. Drain large can pineapple, spread over mixture in pan. Whip cream, sweeten with 2 t. powdered sugar. Spread over mixture. Cover with remaining crumbs. Prepare 24 hours before serving. Chill in refrigerator until ready to serve.

Parsonage Emergency Dessert

2 c. graham cracker crumbs
1 c. milk
1-1/2 c. whipping cream

1 T. sugar
1 t. vanilla
1-1/2 fruit or berry preserves

Soak the crumbs in the milk. Whip the cream and to it add the sugar and vanilla. In a glass dessert dish, layer the crumbs, preserves, and whipped cream in that order. Sprinkle with crumbs.

Rhubarb Shortcake

2 c. raw rhubarb (cut in small cubes)
1-1/2 c. sugar
1 c. sour cream

1 t. baking soda
1/2 t. salt
2 c. flour

Mix rhubarb with 1/2 c. sugar and let stand for 30 minutes. Stir in baking soda into the sour cream, and then combine this mixture with all the other ingredients, including the sweetened rhubarb. Spread in buttered casserole, 9 inch square. Sprinkle with sugar and cinnamon. Dot with butter and bake 30 to 40 minutes at 350°. Serve with sweetened whipped cream or softened vanilla ice cream.

Strawberry Shortcut Cake

1 c. miniature marshmallows
2 c. (2-10 oz. pkg.) frozen sliced
   strawberries in syrup (thawed)
1 pkg. (3 oz.) strawberry
   flavored gelatin
2-1/4 c. Pillsbury flour
1-1/2 c. sugar

1/2 c. shortening
3 t. baking powder
1/2 t. salt
1 c. milk
1/2 t. vanilla
3 eggs

Generously grease bottom of pan, 13 x 9 inch. Sprinkle marshmallows evenly over bottom pan. Thoroughly combine thawed strawberries and syrup with dry gelatin (set aside—no need to sift flour; measure by spooning into cup; leveling off). In large bowl combine remaining ingredients. Blend at low speed until moistened. Beat 3 minutes at medium speed, scraping sides of bowl occasionally.

Pour batter evenly over marshmallows in prepared pan. Spoon strawberry mixture evenly over batter. Bake at 350° for 45 to 50 minutes until golden brown and toothpick inserted in middle comes out clean. Serve warm with ice cream or whipped cream.

Shortcake for Strawberries

2 c. flour
1/2 c. sugar
4 t. baking powder
1/2 t. salt

1/2 t. cream of tartar
1/2 c. margarine
3/4 c. milk

Put dry ingredients in a bowl. Using a pastry blender, cut in margarine. Add milk and mix well. Turn out onto a floured board. Pat about 1 inch thick. Cut into rounds with a cookie cutter. Bake in a 400° oven for 15 minutes or until lightly brown.

No Bake Cheesecake

1 pkg. lemon Jello
1 can evaporated milk or
   pkg. whipping cream

1 8-oz. pkg. cream cheese
1 c. sugar
1 t. vanilla

Dissolve lemon Jello in 2 c. hot water. Chill only until it starts to set. Blend cream cheese with sugar and vanilla. Whip cream and blend all ingredients. Pour in graham cracker lined pan and chill. Can be made the day before.

Bittersweet Chocolate Dessert

Chocolate cookie crumbs
1 c. milk
32 marshmallows
1/4 t. salt

1 t. almond extract
1 pt. whipping cream
2 squares baking chocolate

Melt marshmallows in milk and add salt and extract. Chill. Shave or grate chocolate and whip cream. Combine with chilled mixture. Put cookie crumbs on bottom of flat cake pan. Spread on whipped mixture, top with crumbs and chill several hours.

Mint Dessert

26 Oreo cookies
32 marshmallows
1 c. evaporated milk
1/8 t. salt

1/2 t. peppermint flavoring
Few drops green coloring
1 pt. cream for whipping
    or use Cool Whip

Melt marshmallows and milk in double boiler, add salt, flavoring and coloring. Let cool. Whip cream very stiff and fold in. Crush cookies and put half of crumbs on bottom of well buttered 9 x 13 inch pan. Add filling and top with crumbs. Let stand overnight; cut into squares.

Perfect Baked Custard

6 eggs
1/2 to 3/4 c. sugar
1/2 t. salt

4 c. hot milk
2 t. vanilla

Combine eggs, sugar and salt in mixing bowl. Beat just enough to blend together. Add hot milk slowly and mix well. Stir in vanilla. Pour into 1-1/2 qt. shallow baking pan, 1-1/2 qt. deep casserole or 8 individual custard cups. Place in pan of hot water. Bake in slow oven, 325°, until inserted knife comes out clean. Shallow baking pan—45 minutes; deep casserole—60 minutes; custard cups—30 minutes. Delicious served frosty cold. Makes 6 to 8 servings.

Old Fashioned Shortcake

2 c. flour (sifted)
3 t. baking powder
3/4 t. salt

1/4 c. light brown sugar (firmly packed)
1/2 c. butter or oleo
About 1/2 c. milk

Preheat oven to 450°. Grease an 8 x 1-1/2 inch layer pan. Sift flour, baking powder, and salt into medium bowl. Stir in sugar. With pastry blender, cut in oleo until size of small peas. Make well in center; pour in milk all at once; stir with fork just until dough cleans side of bowl. Add a little more milk, if necessary.

Turn out onto lightly floured surface. Knead very gently 10 times, until light. Pat dough evenly in pan. Bake 20 minutes, until nicely browned. Serve hot, with fresh fruit and whipped cream.

Pumpkin Pie Dessert Squares

1 pkg. yellow cake mix
   (save 1 c. for topping)

1/2 c. oleo (melted)
1 egg

FILLING
1 large can pumpkin pie mix
2 eggs

2/3 c. milk

TOPPING
1 c. reserved cake mix
1/4 c. sugar

1/4 c. oleo
1 t. cinnamon

Mix first 3 ingredients and pat into 9 x 13 inch pan, grease bottom of pan only. Mix the pumpkin pie mix, eggs and milk. Pour over crust. Mix ingredients for the topping and sprinkle over pumpkin filling. Bake 45 to 50 minutes at 350°.

Cherry Dessert

graham cracker crust
2 envelopes whipped topping
1 8 oz. pkg. cream cheese

1 c. powdered sugar
1 t. vanilla
1 can cherry pie filling

Prepare graham cracker crust for 13 x 9 inch pan. Bake 4 minutes at 350°. Cool. Prepare whipped topping according to package instructions. Whip cream cheese, add powdered sugar and vanilla. Add whipped topping to cheese-sugar mixture. Spread on crust. Carefully spread cherry pie filling on top. Refrigerate until serving time.

Raspberry Swirl

3/4 c. graham cracker crumbs
3 T. butter (melted)
2 T. sugar
3 eggs (separated)
1 8-oz. pkg. cream cheese

1 c. sugar
1/8 t. salt
1 c. heavy cream
1 10-oz. pkg. frozen raspberries
 (partially frozen)

Combine thoroughly crumbs, melted butter and 2 T. sugar. Press lightly into well greased 7 x 11 x 1-1/2 inch pan. Bake in moderate oven about 6 minutes. Cool thoroughly.

Beat egg yolks until thick. Add cream cheese, sugar and salt. Beat until smooth and light. Beat egg whites until stiff peaks form. Whip cream stiff and thoroughly fold with egg whites into cheese mixture. In a mixer or blender, crush raspberries to a pulp. Gently swirl half of fruit pulp through cheese filling and spread mixture into crust. Spoon remaining puree over top; swirl with a knife. Freeze, then cover and return to freezer. Makes 6 to 8 servings. This is better made a day ahead. Allow to stand 20 minutes at room temperature before cutting and serving.

Cream Puffs

1/2 c. boiling water
1/4 c. butter

1/2 c. all-purpose flour
2 eggs

Whipped cream, custard, cream filling or ice cream

Pour boiling water over butter in saucepan and bring to boil. Add flour all at once and stir constantly with wooden spoon until mixture leaves the sides of the pan and forms a ball. Remove from heat. Immediately add unbeaten eggs 1 at a time, beating to a smooth paste after each one. Drop by heaping T. onto a greased baking sheet, keeping mounds uniform about 3 inches apart. Bake in a hot oven, 450°, 15 minutes or until well puffed and delicately brown. Then place on cake rack to cool. When cold cut off tops with a sharp knife. Fill with your favorite cream filling, custard, whipped cream or ice cream, and replace tops. Makes 6 to 7 puffs.

Mix the oil of gladness with the vinegar of
sadness so that the sauce of life will be
more palatable.

Jewish Coffee Cake

1 white cake mix
1 pkg. instant vanilla pudding
1/2 c. butter

4 eggs
2 t. vanilla
8 oz. sour cream

SUGAR MIXTURE
MIX:
1/3 c. sugar
1/3 c. nuts

1 t. cocoa
1 t. cinnamon

Mix first section all together in 1 bowl. Beat at high speed for 5 minutes.

Grease tube pan. Pour in half of batter. Sprinkle sugar mixture and cut through with knife (save a little to sprinkle on top of cake). Pour in remaining batter. Bake at 350° for 50-55 minutes. Cool 20 minutes before removing from pan.

Cream Puffs with Mixer

1 c. water
1/2 c. butter or margarine

1 c. all-purpose flour
4 eggs

Heat oven to 400°. In a small saucepan, heat water and butter to a rolling boil. Stir in flour (with a wooden spoon) until mixture forms a ball, 1 minute.

Remove from heat. Cool a bit. Using a mixer, beat in eggs all at one time. Continue beating until mixture is smooth. Drop dough by scant 1/4 cupfuls three inches apart on an ungreased baking sheet. Bake 35-40 minutes or until puffed and golden brown. Cool away from drafts. Cut off tops with a sharp knife. Fill each with 1/3 c. of pudding or whipped cream. Replace top. Makes 12.

Homemade Strawberry Ice Cream

1 10-oz. pkg. sliced frozen strawberries
1 T. lemon juice

1/2 pt. whipping cream
2/3 c. sweetened condensed milk

Thaw berries in mixing bowl, add lemon juice. Stir in sweetened condensed milk. Whip cream, fold into melted strawberry mixture. Freeze in ice cube tray. Stir several times while freezing. Serves 6 to 8.

Heavenly Fruit Hash

1 No. 2-1/2 can fruit cocktail (drained)   1 c. miniature marshmallows
1 or 2 bananas (sliced)   1/2 c. seeded grapes (halved)
2 T. sugar   1/2 c. whipping cream (whipped)

Combine fruit, sugar, and marshmallows. Fold in whipped cream and keep chilled until serving.

Boysenberry Dessert

1/2 lb. marshmallows   1 c. whipping cream
1/2 c. milk   1 No. 2 can boysenberries
2 T. cornstarch

GRAHAM CRACKER CRUST

1-1/2 c. graham cracker crumbs   1/3 c. sugar
1/2 c. butter

Melt marshmallows in milk. Cool. Whip cream, fold into above mixture. Strain juice from berries, add cornstarch to juice. Cook until thickened. Cool, then fold in berries. Make crust with crumbs, sugar, and butter. Butter an 8 x 10 inch pan. Put in layer of crumbs, then a layer of marshmallow filling, then a layer of berry filling (using all) then a layer of marshmallow filling. Top with crumbs and chill. Can be made a day before serving. Must be refrigerated.

Pumpkin Rice Pudding

1 16-oz. can pumpkin   1/2 t. ginger
3/4 c. sugar   1/4 t. cloves
1/2 t. salt   2 eggs (slightly beaten)
1 t. cinnamon   1 14-oz. can evaporated milk
1/2 c. raisins   2/3 c. precooked rice
Whipped cream and candied fruit for garnish

In mixing bowl combine sugar, pumpkin, salt and spices. Stir in eggs. Add evaporated milk, mix well. Stir in rice and raisins. Pour into 1-1/2 qt. casserole. Place casserole in pan, filling pan with water to depth of 1 inch. Bake in 350° oven for 15 minutes. Stir mixture until well combined. Bake 50 to 60 minutes more or until knife comes out clean when inserted in pudding. Top with dollop of whipped cream and tiny piece of candied fruit for color.

Lemon Delight

1/2 lb. vanilla wafers
1 c. Borden's Eagle Brand milk
cherries (optional)

2 lemons
1/2 pt. whipping cream or
1 pkg. Dream Whip

Crush wafers and put 1/2 crumbs on bottom of 10 inch square pan. Mix lemon juice with milk until smooth and thick. Then spread mixture over crumbs. Whip cream, add a little sugar. Spread over the milk mixture. Top with remainder of crumbs and let stand in refrigerator overnight. Cut in serving pieces. Whipped cream and a cherry may be placed on each piece or leave plain.

Cranberry Dessert

2 c. cranberries
1 large or 2 small bananas
2/3 c. sugar
2-3 c. crushed vanilla wafers
1/2 c. oleo

1 c. powdered sugar
2 eggs
1/2 c. nuts (chopped)
1 c. whipping cream

Combine cranberries, chopped or ground, bananas and sugar. Set aside. Place 1/2 cookie crumbs in 8 x 8 inch pan. Cream oleo, sugar, beat in eggs. Spread over crumbs. Top with cranberry mixture. Spread with nuts and cream which has been whipped. Sprinkle on remaining crumbs and chill 4 hours or overnight. Cut in squares to serve.

Coconut Crunch

MIX:
1/2 c. soft butter
1 c. flour

1/4 c. brown sugar
1 c. Angel Flake coconut

FILLING:
1 pkg. cooked vanilla pudding

Cream, whipped

Spread crunch mixture on cookie sheet and bake at 350°. Stir occasionally and watch carefully so it does not burn. Bake until golden brown. Cool.

Prepare Filling: Spread 1/2 of crunch in 9 inch square pan. Spread vanilla pudding over bottom layer. On top of pudding, put layer of cream, whipped. Sprinkle rest of crunch on top. Chill and serve.

Raspberry Cream

1 pkg. raspberry Jello
1 c. boiling water

1 10-oz. pkg. frozen strawberries
1/2 pt. vanilla ice cream

Dissolve gelatin in water, stir in berries and ice cream. Refrigerate about 20 minutes, spoon into 4 serving dishes.

Strawberry Sherbet

1 pt. strawberries
   (washed and hulled)
2 T. lemon juice
1/2 c. sugar

1/4 c. light corn syrup
1/8 t. salt
2 egg whites
1 c. Cool Whip (thawed)

Place strawberries and lemon juice into blender container. Cover and blend until smooth. Pour into bowl, stir in sugar, corn syrup and salt. In medium sized bowl, beat egg whites stiff. Fold into strawberry mixture, smoothly. Fold in whipped topping well. Pour into 1-1/2 qt. freezer container. Cover, freeze until firm, about 3 hours. Remove from freezer 10 minutes before serving. Makes about 8 to 10 servings.

Country Vanilla Ice Cream

4 eggs
2-1/4 c. sugar
5 c. milk

4 c. cream
4-1/2 t. vanilla extract
1/2 t. salt

To beaten eggs, gradually add sugar. Beat until very stiff. Add remaining ingredients and mix thoroughly. Pour into freezer and freeze; makes 1 gallon of ice cream.

Strawberry Delight Dessert

1 pkg. strawberry gelatin
1 c. boiling water
1 pkg. frozen strawberries

1 pkg. Dream Whip or other whipped topping
1 3-oz. pkg. cream cheese
1 c. miniature marshmallows

Add gelatin to boiling water. When dissolved add frozen strawberries. Stir until strawberries are thawed. Place in refrigerator until gelatin is set. Beat topping, omitting vanilla, until thick (according to package directions). Add cream cheese and marshmallows. Mix well. Spread over gelatin. Yield: 8 servings.

Prune Whip

pinch of salt
3 egg whites
1/3 c. sugar
1/2 t. vanilla extract or lemon juice

1 c. stewed prunes (drained;
    cut fine; stones removed)
1/2 t. cinnamon

Add salt to egg whites and beat until almost stiff. Then add sugar slowly and continue beating until whites are stiff. Fold in remaining ingredients, turn into a greased 1-1/2 qt. baking dish, and bake in a slow oven, 350°, for 20-25 minutes. Serve cold with cream. Serves 6.

Raisin-Rice Pudding

1-1/2 c. cooked rice
3/4 c. raisins
2 eggs (beaten)
1/2 c. sugar
1 t. vanilla

1/4 t. salt
1/2 t. cinnamon
1/2 t. nutmeg
2 c. milk (scalded)

Combine all ingredients except milk; then gradually stir in milk, stirring constantly. Pour into 1-1/2 qt. casserole. Bake in moderate oven, 350°, 1 hour or until knife inserted into pudding comes out clean.

Mrs. Gerke's Rice Pudding

1 qt. milk
1 c. cooked rice
1/2 c. sugar
4 egg yolks (beaten)

3 T. cornstarch dissolved in 1/3 c. milk
1 t. vanilla
4 egg whites (beaten until stiff)
1/2 c. sugar

Combine milk, 1/2 c. sugar, egg yolks, cornstarch dissolved in milk. Cook over slow heat, stirring constantly until thickened. Stir in cooked rice.

Remove from heat and add vanilla. Beat egg whites and 1/2 c. sugar to make meringue. Place custard mixture in a baking dish. Carefully place the meringue on top of the custard, being careful to seal all the edges. Place baking dish in 325° oven for 25 minutes. This is best served warm.

Quick Apple Dessert

1/2 c. sugar
1/4 c. tapioca
1/2 t. cinnamon
1/4 t. nutmeg

2 c. water
1 lemon (grated rind and juice)
2 T. butter
1 can sliced pie apples (or cook your own)

Combine sugar, tapioca, cinnamon, nutmeg, and water. Cook, stirring until mixture boils. Remove from heat. Add butter, lemon juice and rind. Cool 15 minutes; stir; add apple slices. Serve warm with cream.

Banana Split Dessert

1 can crushed pineapple
2 pkg. Lucky Whip
2 c. graham cracker crumbs
3/4 lb. oleo
2 c. powdered sugar

2 eggs
bananas
nuts (chopped)
maraschino cherries

Drain pineapple and set aside. Prepare Lucky Whip according to package directions. Mix graham cracker crumbs with 1/4 lb. oleo. Spread into 9 x 13 inch pan and bake at 400° for 10 minutes or until light brown. Mix 1/2 lb. oleo with powdered sugar and eggs, beating for 20 minutes at medium speed. Spread over cooled crust. Slice bananas the long way and place on pudding mixture. Sprinkle on pineapple and cover with Lucky Whip. Sprinkle with chopped nuts and maraschino cherries. Chill.

Pie Filling Dessert

40 soda crackers (crushed)
1 stick oleo (melted)
1 can pie filling (berry)
1/2 c. milk

4 egg whites (beaten)
1 c. sugar
1 envelope Dream Whip
1 t. vanilla

Mix crackers and oleo. Pat into 9 x 13 inch pan. Beat egg whites and add sugar. Whip until stiff. Carefully spread over crust. Bake at 350° for 15 minutes. Cool. Spread filling over it. Prepare Dream Whip. Spread over pie filling. Refrigerate until serving time. Cut into squares.

Baked Apple Pancake

4 eggs
1-1/2 c. milk
1/2 t. salt
2 T. sugar
2 c. flour

3 tart apples (sliced)
3 T. butter or oleo
1/2 to 1 c. sugar mixed with
   1 t. cinnamon

Beat the eggs until thick, then add the milk, salt, and sugar. Then mix in the flour, well. Let batter stand for 30 minutes. Meanwhile, prepare the apples. Butter well two 9 inch round cake pans and sprinkle with remaining cinnamon-sugar and dot with butter. Pour batter over apples. Bake 375° for 30 minutes or until golden and set. Serve hot immediately or reheat before serving.

Easy Cherry Dessert

1 can cherry pie filling
3/4 c. pancake mix

1/4 c. brown sugar
1/4 c. butter or oleo

Pour pie filling into 8 inch square pan. Combine pancake mix and brown sugar. Sprinkle over cherry base. Melt butter or oleo and drizzle over the top. Bake at 375° for 30 minutes. Serve warm with vanilla ice cream.

Raspberry Dessert

2 10-oz. pkg. frozen red raspberries
1 c. water
1/2 c. sugar
2 t. lemon juice
4 T. cornstarch
1/4 c. cold water
50 large marshmallows

1 c. milk
2 c. heavy cream (whipped) or
   2 pkg. dessert topping mix
1-1/4 c. graham cracker crumbs
1/4 c. nuts (chopped)
1/4 c. butter (melted)

Heat raspberries with water, sugar and lemon juice. Dissolve cornstarch in cold water, stir into raspberries and cook until thickened and clear. Cool.

Melt marshmallows in milk over boiling water and cool thoroughly.

Whip cream or dessert topping mix and fold into marshmallow mixture. Mix graham cracker crumbs, nuts and butter in a 13 x 9 x 5/8 inch pan. Press firmly into bottom of pan. Spread marshmallow-cream mixture over crumbs. Spread raspberry mixture over top. Chill until firm. Serves 15-18.

Strawberry Torte

1 3-oz. pkg. strawberry Jello
1 c. boiling water
1 pkg. frozen strawberries
Graham cracker crust

1 c. whipping cream
1/2 c. sugar
2 t. vanilla

Combine Jello, water and strawberries, let almost jell. Whip cream, fold in sugar and vanilla. Fold all together and put on a graham cracker crust.

Cherry Cheese Cakes

1 c. vanilla wafers crumbs
2 t. lemon juice
1/2 t. vanilla
3 or 4 T. butter (melted)

8 oz. pkg. cream cheese
1/3 c.sugar
1 egg
1 lb. can red pie cherries

Line 12 muffin cups with paper bake cups. Combine cookie crumbs and melted butter and mix well. Spoon about 1 T. crumb mix into bottom of each bake cup and press gently. Beat cream cheese until fluffy. Add sugar, egg, lemon juice and vanilla and beat until smooth. Pour evenly into each crumb lined paper and bake at 375° for 15 minutes. Cool thoroughly. Spoon cherry pie mix on each cheese cake.

Canned Peach Cobbler

1/2 c. sugar
1 T. cornstarch
2-1/2 c. canned peaches and juice
Butter & cinnamon
3 T. shortening

1/2 c. milk
1 c. flour (sifted)
1 T. sugar
1-1/2 t. baking powder
1/2 t. salt

Mix in saucepan 1/2 c. sugar and cornstarch, stir in gradually peaches and juice. Bring to a boil and boil 1 minute, stirring constantly. Pour into 1-1/2 qt. baking dish and dot with butter, sprinkle with cinnamon. Sift together flour, 1 T. sugar, baking powder and salt; cut in shortening with pastry blender or 2 knives until mixture looks like meal. Stir in milk, drop by spoonful onto hot fruit. Bake at 400° for 25 to 30 minutes, until golden brown. Serve warm with juice and cream. 6 to 8 servings.

Apple Kuchen

1/2 c. butter	1/2 c. sugar
1/2 c. coconut	1 t. cinnamon
1 pkg. yellow cake mix	1 c. dairy sour cream
1 can pie sliced apples	2 egg yolks or 1 egg
or 2-1/2 c. sliced cooking apples	

Heat oven to 350°. Cut butter into dry cake mix until crumbly. Add coconut. Pat mixture lightly into ungreased pan 9 x 13 inches. Bake 10 minutes. Arrange apple slices on warm crust. Mix sugar and cinnamon, sprinkle on apples. Blend sour cream and egg, drizzle over apples. (Will not completely cover apples). Bake 25 minutes, until edges are light brown. Do not over bake. Serve warm. 12 to 15 servings.

Apple Goo

2 medium apples	2 T. flour
3/4 c. sugar	1 t. baking powder
1/2 c. nuts (chopped)	1/8 t. salt
1/2 c. dates (cut in pieces)	1 egg (unbeaten)

Pare, core, and dice apples fine. Add sugar, nuts and dates; mix with flour, baking powder and salt (sifted together). Drop egg into mixture, blend. Place in greased 8 inch baking dish, bake in moderate oven 350° for about 20 minutes or until golden brown on top. Serve with cream, ice cream, or whipped cream. Serves 4-6.

Spicy Pumpkin Freeze

1 c. pumpkin	1/2 t. nutmeg
1/2 c. sugar	1/2 c. nuts (chopped)
1/2 t. salt	1 qt. vanilla ice cream
1/2 t. ginger	Gingersnaps
1/2 t. cinnamon	

Soften ice cream slightly. Line 11 x 7 inch pan with 16 gingersnaps. Combine all but gingersnaps. Spread half on gingersnaps in pan, top with more gingersnaps and top with remaining mix. Freeze. Cut in squares to serve.

Eclairs

1/2 c. butter	4 eggs
1 c. water	1 c. flour

Add butter to water and bring to boil. Add flour. Beat well until flour leaves side of bowl. Remove from stove. Add eggs, 1 at a time, beating continually. Then with a spoon or pastry tube, shape dough into oblongs, 1 inch x 3 inches. Bake on a greased sheet in 450° oven for 15 minutes, then reduce heat to 350°, bake about 30 minutes longer. Cool and fill with vanilla cream filling made as follows:

2 c. milk	2 eggs
5 T. flour	1/2 c. sugar
1/4 t. salt	2 t. vanilla

Scald 1-1/2 c. milk in double boiler. Stir 1/2 c. cold milk into the flour and salt, making a smooth paste. Stir this into the hot milk. Continue to stir until mixture thickens. Cover and let cook for 15 minutes. Beat eggs, add sugar and beat again. Stir egg mixture into the hot mixture and cook two minutes. When cool, add the vanilla.

French Glaze Pie, Raspberry or Blueberry

CRUST

1/2 c. oleo	1 c. flour
2 T. sugar	

FILLING

1 qt. berries (fresh or canned)	3 T. cornstarch
1 c. sugar	

Crust—Cream oleo and sugar. Add flour, mix and press into pan. Bake 375° 12 to 15 minutes or until golden brown.

Filling—Crush berries to make 1-1/2 c. Add water if necessary. Bring to boiling and gradually add sugar mixed with cornstarch. Cook and stir until thickened. Pour in baked shell and chill for 2 hours. May be served with whipped topping mix.

As a white candle in a holy place,
So is the beauty of an aged face.
J. Campbell

Apple-Sour Cream Bake

1-1/2 c. all-purpose flour
1/2 c. sugar
2 t. baking powder
1/2 t. salt
1/2 t. cinnamon
1/2 c. milk
1/4 c. soft butter

1 egg
1 c. tart apples (diced)
1/2 c. sour cream
1 egg (slightly beaten)
1/4 c. sugar
1/3 c. walnuts (chopped)

Sift together dry ingredients. Add milk, butter, and unbeaten egg, beat until smooth. Stir in apples. Pour into greased 9 inch baking pan. Blend sour cream and slightly beaten egg; spread over batter. Sprinkle with mixture of sugar and walnuts. Bake in 375° oven for 30 minutes. Cut in 8 or 9 inch squares. Serve warm.

Marshmallow Whip

No. 2-1/2 can fruit cocktail
16 marshmallows
1/4 t. salt

3 oz. cream cheese
1 c. whipping cream

CRUMB CRUST
1/4 c. melted butter
1/4 c. sugar

16 graham crackers, crushed

Drain fruit cocktail, put 2 T. of juice in saucepan. Add marshmallows, heat slowly, stirring constantly, until marshmallows are melted. Add fruit and salt. Blend the cheese with enough cream to make it consistency of mayonnaise. Whip remaining cream stiff. Fold cheese and cream into fruit mixture. Pour over crumb crust in 9 x 13 inch pan. Top with remaining crumbs. Chill.

Real joy comes not from ease or riches or from the praise of men, but from doing something worthwhile.

Wilfred T. Grenfell

Cherry Pastry

3-1/2 c. flour	2 T. sugar
1 c. margarine	1 dry yeast
1/2 t. salt	3 egg yolks
2/3 c. milk	2 cans cherry pie filling

Mix flour, margarine and salt until crumbly. Make well in middle and set aside. Scald and cool milk, add sugar, egg yolks and yeast. Pour into flour mixture and mix until dough no longer sticks to hands. Divide dough in half—roll to fit jelly roll pan 10 x 15 inches. Spread with cherry filling, top with second half of dough, let rise 1 hour, bake at 350° for 35 to 40 minutes. Drizzle with thin powdered sugar icing while slightly warm.

Rainbow Torte

3 pkg. Jello (3 flavors)	2 pkg. gelatin
1 pt. whipping cream	1/4 c. cold water
1 c. powdered sugar	1/4 c. boiling water
1 small can crushed pineapple	jelly roll or lady fingers

Make three colors or flavors Jello in separate flat pans using 1-1/2 c. water instead of 2. Set. Cut into small cubes. Line a spring form or angel food pan with slices of jelly roll or lady fingers (sides and bottom). Whip cream and add sugar and pulp of can of pineapple. Dissolve unflavored gelatin in cold water. Add boiling water and pineapple juice. Mix into whipped cream. Fold in Jello cubes. Pour into jelly roll lined pan. Refrigerate several hours. Turn out on large plate to serve.

Gratitude

For singing kettles and warm lamp glow,
For winter moon on clean white snow,
For purple dusk and stars hung low,
  I thank Thee.

For rippling river and singing seas,
For brief sweet blooms and tall dark trees,
For crimson birds and small brown bees,
  I thank Thee.

For all Thy love in lavish measure,
For all the peace of homely pleasure,
For all Thy gifts of boundless treasurer,
  I thank Thee.

Marie E. Baxter

Salads and Dressings

Orange Salad Mold

1 pkg. orange Jello
3/4 c. boiling water
1/4 c. sugar
1 c. cottage cheese
1 c. whipping cream

1 small can crushed pineapple
   (undrained)
1 c. mandarin oranges
   (drained)

Mix Jello and boiling water to dissolve. Cool until partially jelled. Whip cream. Add all ingredients to jelled mixture and pour into mold to jell.

Spicy Apricot Mold

1 can unpeeled apricot
   halves (or 2 c.)
1 c. pineapple tidbits
2 T. vinegar
1 t. whole cloves

4 inches stick cinnamon
2 3-oz. pkgs. orange gelatin
3/4 c. boiling water
3/4 c. apricot nectar
1/2 c. dairy sour cream

Drain apricots and pineapple, reserving syrup. Combine syrups; add vinegar and spices. Bring to boil. Simmer 10 minutes, strain syrup, add hot water to measure 2 c. Pour over 1 pkg. orange Jello, stir until dissolved. Chill until partially set. Fold in well drained apricots and pineapple. Pour into 6 cup mold. Chill until almost firm. Meanwhile dissolve second package Jello in 3/4 c. boiling water, stir in apricot juice. Chill until partially set; whip until fluffy. Swirl in sour cream. Pour over first layer. Chill at least 8 hours. Serves 8 to 10.

Raspberry Salad

2 small pkg. raspberry Jello
3 c. hot water
1 pkg. frozen raspberries
2 bananas (mashed)

1 medium can crushed pineapple
   (drained)
1 small carton sour cream

Dissolve Jello in the hot water. Add the pkg. of frozen raspberries and the juice from it, while raspberries are still frozen. When the Jello and raspberries start to set, add the mashed bananas and the drained pineapple. Put half of this mixture in a mold and let set until firm. Spread sour cream over this. Then pour remainder of Jello mixture over the sour cream and refrigerate until firm.

Spring Carrot Salad

1/2 c. raisins
2 c. carrot (finely grated)
1/3 c. dairy sour cream
1 T. lemon juice

1/2 t. lemon rind
2 t. sugar
1/2 t. salt
Lettuce

Cover raisins with boiling water, let stand for 5 minutes. Drain and cool thoroughly. Combine raisins and carrots. Blend sour cream, lemon juice and rind, sugar and salt. Mix lightly with carrots and raisins. Serve immediately on lettuce. 4 to 5 servings.

Bean and Pea Salad

1 can French style green beans
1 can small peas
1 green pepper

2 stalks celery
1 small onion
1 can pimento

Drain beans and peas. Place in a medium sized bowl. Slice onions, add to vegetables. Chop up remaining ingredients. Add to vegetables. Add dressing. Refrigerate several hours before serving.

DRESSING

1/2 c. salad oil
1-1/2 c. sugar
1 T. water

paprika
1 c. vinegar
1 T. salt

Mix all ingredients. Stir well to dissolve sugar.

Bunny Salad *(One Serving Salad)*

lettuce leaf
1 pear half (chilled)
2 raisins

1 red cinnamon candy
2 blanched almonds
1 cottage cheese ball

Place a nice crisp lettuce leaf on plate. Place chilled pear half upside down on lettuce. Make bunny with narrow end for face. Eyes, use 2 raisins; for nose, cinnamon candy; for ears, 2 almonds; and for tail, form a cottage cheese ball.

Mandarin Orange Mold

2 pkg. orange Jello
1 c. hot water
1 small can frozen concentrate
   orange juice

1 pt. vanilla ice cream
   (softened)
1 can mandarin orange slices

Dissolve Jello in hot water. Mix in orange juice and add softened ice cream. Mix in drained orange slices. Let set.

Garden Salad

1 pkg. lime Jello
Let set, then whip.

1-1/2 c. boiling water

ADD:
1/2 c. salad dressing
1 c. cottage cheese

1/2 c. whipped cream or
   topping mix

Mix well and add 1 T. each of grated carrot, chopped onion, cucumber, green pepper, and celery. Pour into greased mold, refrigerate until set. Unmold on lettuce.

Russian Dressing

1 c. oil
1/2 c. sugar
5 T. vinegar or lemon juice

1 c. catsup
1 t. onion (grated)
1/2 t. celery seed (optional)

Beat oil and sugar together for 5 minutes or spin in blender 1 to 2 minutes. Add remaining to mix.

Maurice Salad

lettuce (shredded)
ham (shredded)
chicken (shredded)

cheese (Swiss, or brick; shredded)
sweet gherkins (shredded)

DRESSING

1/2 pt. sour cream
1/2 pt. salad dressing
1 T. chives (chopped)
1 T. vinegar

1 T. sugar
salt and pepper
2 hard boiled eggs (sieved)

Cut in small pieces boiled ham, cooked chicken, cheese and sweet pickles. Serve tossed on shredded lettuce. Mix all the ingredients for dressing and chill. Pour on dressing individually as you serve salad with hot rolls for dinner. This dressing really makes the salad.

Ceil's Salad Dressing

1 can tomato soup
1/4 c. oil
1 t. dry mustard
1 t. paprika

3/4 c. vinegar
1/2 c. sugar
1 t. salt
1 c. onion (chopped)

Combine all ingredients. Mix well in blender or by hand. Store tightly covered in refrigerator. Keeps for several weeks.

"Red Cedar" Salad Dressing

2 c. oil
1 c. wine vinegar
1 clove garlic (minced)
1 c. chili sauce

2 T. onion (small, grated)
2 T. lemon juice
1 c. sugar

Mix all ingredients, shake well and use. Garlic is optional.

An apology is a good way to have the last word.

Margaret's Chefs Dressing

1/4 clove garlic
1 T. salt
1 T. prepared mustard
1 egg

8 T. vinegar
A few drops artificial sweetener
1/2 c. water
2 c. oil

Mix garlic and salt in bowl. Add mustard, egg, sweetener, and 3 T. of the vinegar. Beat thoroughly. Gradually add remaining vinegar, beating well. Add water and oil and beat. Makes 3 cups.

German Potato Salad

5 slices bacon
2 T. flour
1/3 c. sugar
2 t. salt
1/8 t. pepper
1/4 c. vinegar

1/4 c. lemon juice
1 c. water
1 qt. potatoes (cooked; sliced)
1/4 c. onions (sliced)
1/4 c. celery (diced)
1 t. parsley flakes

Fry bacon, remove bacon and keep 1/4 c. fat in skillet. Add flour, sugar, salt, pepper, and blend together. Add vinegar, lemon juice and water. Cook until thick, add crumbled bacon, parsley flakes, onion, celery, and mix with potatoes. Serve warm.

Beet-Herring Salad

2 medium potatoes
4 carrots
2 c. beets
1 small onion

2 dill pickles (diced)
2 tart apples (optional)
3/4 c. pickled herring, sardines,
    or anchovies (diced)

Cook, peel and dice the vegetables. Combine all ingredients together. Sprinkle with vinegar to taste. Salad may also be made without the fish.

Tuna Salad

1 can tuna fish
1/2 c. nuts (chopped)
3 hard cooked eggs
1/2 c. celery (chopped)

1/2 small onion (chopped)
1 T. lemon juice
1/2 c. mayonnaise

Combine and toss all ingredients and serve on a bed of lettuce.

Korean Salad

DRESSING

1/2 c. salad oil
1/2 c. apple cider vinegar
3/4 c. sugar

1-1/2 t. salt
1 medium onion (chopped)
1/3 c. catsup

SALAD

2 pkg. fresh spinach
1 can water chestnuts (cut up)
1 can bean sprouts (drained)

2 hard cooked eggs (cut up)
6 strips bacon (fried crisp,
    crumbled)

Dressing—Combine ingredients and shake. Make ahead of time and refrigerate.

Salad—Wash spinach ahead of time, wrap in towel, refrigerate. Toss spinach with other ingredients and pour dressing over salad just before serving. Serves 8-10 adults.

Twin Cheese Salad

2 pkgs. lemon Jello
1 c. boiling water
2 c. liquid from pear halves
2 c. cottage cheese

2 c. yellow cheese (shredded)
2 c. canned pears (diced)
1 tub Cool Whip

Dissolve Jello in boiling water. Stir in pear liquid. Chill until partially set. Fold in cottage cheese, yellow shredded cheese, diced pears, and Cool Whip. Pour into mold or large pan, which has been oiled or dipped in cool water.

Pink Lady Salad

1 (8 oz.) cream cheese
1/4 c. cherry juice
1 carton cream, whipped
Cherries and coconut for garnish

1 small can crushed pineapple
1 small can fruit cocktail
2 apples (cut up)

Blend cream cheese and cherry juice. Add whipped cream and mix. Combine pineapple, fruit cocktail and apples. Add to whipped cream mixture. Garnish with cherries and coconut.

Cottage Cheese Salad *(Large Quantity)*

1 qt. carton cottage cheese
1 c. crushed pineapple (drained)
2 c. marshmallows (plain or colored)
1/2 pt. whipping cream
1 small bottle maraschino cherries

Mix cottage cheese, crushed pineapple, and marshmallows. Fold in whipped cream. Place in salad bowl, decorate with maraschino cherries and refrigerate.

Jello Salad

1 box lime Jello
1 c. hot water
Dream Whip or Cool Whip
1 pkg. cream cheese
Small can crushed pineapple (drained)

Dissolve cheese in hot Jello, beat, let jell, beat again. Add Dream Whip or Cool Whip and drained crushed pineapple. Place in mold. Refrigerate.

Church Supper Salad

1 large Cool Whip
1 pkg. fruit flavored gelatin
1 small can crushed pineapple, drained
1 1-lb. carton small curd cottage cheese

Mix dry gelatin, thawed Cool Whip, pineapple and cottage cheese (do not add water to gelatin). Place in mold or serving bowl. Refrigerate several hours or overnight. Orange-pineapple flavored gelatin is nice in this recipe.

Potato Salad Supreme

2 envelopes Knox gelatin
1/2 c. cold water
3 c. mayonnaise
10 c. potatoes (diced, cooked)
2 c. celery (diced)
1 c. green pepper (diced)
2 c. radishes (sliced)
1 c. cucumber (chopped)
1/4 c. onion (chopped)
10 hard boiled eggs (chopped)
4 T. parsley flakes
1-1/2 t. salt
pepper

Soften gelatin in cold water. Dissolve over hot water. Blend in mayonnaise. Combine remaining ingredients and toss with dressing mixture. Press into oiled tube pan, unmold on lettuce. Chill thoroughly several hours or overnight before unmolding. Serves 20 to 30.

Applesauce Salad

1 pkg. lemon Jello
1 c. hot water
2/3 c. thick applesauce

1/2 t. salt
1 c. cottage cheese

Dissolve the Jello in the boiling water. Add applesauce, cottage cheese and salt when Jello begins to thicken. Serve with or without dressing. If the applesauce is thin decrease the amount of water.

Sea Foam Salad

1 (No. 2-1/2) can pears
1 pkg. lime Jello
6 oz. cream cheese

1 c. cream (whipped) or
  1 pkg. Dream Whip
2 T. cream

Drain juice from pears. Heat 1 c. of juice to boiling point. Pour over Jello and stir until dissolved. Cool. Mix cheese and 2 T. cream until smooth. Add Jello mixture, and beat with electric mixer until blended. Chill until almost thickened. Fold in well drained mashed pears and whipped cream. Chill until firm.

Marinated Cole Slaw

1 cabbage
4 onions
1 c. vinegar
1 t. dry mustard

1 t. celery seed
3/4 c. sugar
1-1/2 t. salt
1 c. oil

Slice cabbage and onions very thin; alternate in a casserole. Heat together other ingredients; boil; then add oil. Boil again and pour over cabbage and onions. Cover, let stand at least 24 hours. Will last 10 days in refrigerator.

Cabbage Salad—Austrian Style

4 c. shredded cabbage
1-1/2 T. vinegar
1/2 t. salt

1/4 t. black pepper
1 t. sugar
1/2 t. caraway seed

Combine all ingredients and toss together lightly. Refrigerate for 30 minutes or until ready to serve. Makes 6 servings.

Marinated Cabbage Slaw

1 large head cabbage	1 c. vinegar
1 diced green pepper	1-1/2 c. sugar or 10 envelopes
1 medium onion (cut fine)	Sweet and Low and 3/4 c. sugar
1/2 c. salad oil	1 T. salt

Bring the salad oil, vinegar, sugar and salt to a boil and pour while boiling hot over cabbage, pepper and onion. Cover and let set overnight in refrigerator.

Sauerkraut Salad

2 c. sauerkraut (1 lb. can)	1/2 c. green pepper (thin strips)
1/2 c. sugar	1/2 c. carrot (shredded)
1/2 c. celery (thinly sliced)	1/4 c. onion (chopped)

Cut sauerkraut strands in shorter pieces with scissors. Stir in sugar and let stand 1/2 hour. (Sauerkraut may first be rinsed with cold water and drained well before using.) Add remaining ingredients. Cover bowl tightly and chill in refrigerator at least 12 hours before serving. Makes 8 servings of 1/2 cup.

Corned Beef Salad

1 c. corned beef	1 onion
1 green pepper	1 T. lemon juice
1 c. celery	1 c. salad dressing
1/2 t. salt	1 t. sugar
1/2 c. nuts	1 pkg. lemon Jello

Jell lemon Jello until slightly thickened, add salad dressing and mix in all ingredients. Stir and chill.

Cauliflower Salad

1 head of lettuce, torn into pieces	1-1/2 T. sugar
1 head of cauliflower, cut up	1 lb. crisp bacon
1 bunch green onions, chopped	1/4 c. parmesan cheese
1 small pkg. frozen peas	1 c. Hellman's mayonnaise

Toss together all greens. Add sugar to mayonnaise and spread on top of salad. Top with bacon and cheese. Set in refrigerator overnite. Toss when ready to serve.

Sour Cream Potato Salad

6 c. potatoes (diced, cooked)
3 T. green onions (chopped)
3/4 t. celery seed
1-1/2 t. salt
1/2 t. pepper
4 hard cooked eggs

1 c. sour cream
1/2 c. mayonnaise
1/4 c. vinegar
1 t. prepared mustard
3/4 c. cucumber (diced; optional)

Combine potatoes, onions, celery seed, salt, and pepper. Toss lightly. Separate whites from yolks and chop; add to potato mixture. Mash yolks, add sour cream, mayonnaise, vinegar, and mustard, mix well. Pour over potatoes, toss lightly. Let stand 20 minutes. If desired, add cucumbers just before serving.

Cold Meat Salad

2 c. meat (beef or pork; diced, cooked)
1 c. Pascal celery (sliced)
1 c. tart apples (diced, pared)
1/4 c. mayonnaise

1 T. prepared mustard
1/2 t. salt
crisp lettuce

Combine meat, celery and apple. Mix mayonnaise thoroughly with mustard and salt. Add to meat mixture and toss lightly until all pieces are well coated with dressing. Serve on lettuce leaves. Makes 5 servings.

Easy Dieters' French Dressing

1 can tomato soup
2 T. Sucaryl solution
1/2 c. soybean oil
1/2 c. vinegar
1 t. salt

1 t. garlic (chopped)
1 large onion (sliced thin)
1/4 c. prepared mustard
1/2 t. paprika

Combine all ingredients; mix well. Store in tightly covered jar in the refrigerator. Makes 3 cups.

Nothing so needs reforming as other people's habits.

Basic French Dressing

3/4 c. salad oil
1/4 c. vinegar
1 t. salt
1 t. sugar

1/2 t. paprika
1/4 t. dry mustard
Dash of ground pepper

Combine ingredients in glass jar with a tight fitting cover. Shake until thoroughly blended. Chill. Shake well each time before using. Makes 1 cup of dressing.

VARIATIONS

To basic recipe add:

Tomato Dressing—2 T. catsup and 1/2 t. grated onion

Garlic—1 peeled, quartered clove of garlic. Remove before serving.

Herb—Use lemon juice in place of vinegar. Omit paprika and dry mustard. Add 1/4 t. thyme, 1/2 t. oregano, and 1 t. parsley flakes.

Roquefort—1/4 c. crumbled Roquefort cheese and a few drops onion juice.

Dressing for Tossed Salads

1 c. salad oil
1/2 c. vinegar
1/2 c. water
1 c. sugar

1 T. salt
1 large carrot
1 large onion
1 large green pepper

Place first 5 ingredients in a jar. Grind remaining and add to first. Keeps indefinitely in refrigerator.

Cooked Salad Dressing

1/4 c. sugar
2 T. flour
1 t. salt
1 t. dry mustard

4 egg yolks (beaten)
1/4 c. butter (melted)
1-1/2 c. milk
1/3 c. vinegar

Combine dry ingredients in top of double boiler. Add the egg yolks, butter, and milk and blend well. Gradually add the vinegar. Cook over hot water, stirring constantly until thick. Chill. A delicious dressing for cole slaw or potato salad. Makes 2-1/2 cups.

Tuna Gelatin Salad-Ring

2 (3 oz.) pkg. lime Jello
1 can tuna fish
1 c. celery (diced)

Onion (1/4 c. or more, diced)
1 c. salad dressing
1 ring mold (lightly oiled)

Dissolve Jello using 3 c. water for 2 pkg. Pour some Jello into Jello mold to partially set. Mix tuna, celery, onion and salad dressing with the remaining Jello. When the plain Jello in the mold has set enough that you can spoon the tuna mixture onto it without it sinking into the Jello, put the remaining tuna in the mold and place in the refrigerator to set. Unmold when ready, on a lettuce lined plate. Fill the center of the mold with cottage cheese if desired. Serve with Ritz crackers for a luncheon.

Sour Cream Cole Slaw

1/2 c. sour cream
3 T. vinegar
3 T. sugar
1/2 c. mayonnaise

1/2 t. salt
pepper
3 c. cabbage (chopped)
onion (if preferred)

Combine all ingredients and pour over finely shredded cabbage and onion. Chill. Makes several servings.

Pork-Apple Salad

1-1/2 c. pork (diced, cooked)
1-1/2 c. apple (diced, unpeeled)
1 T. lemon juice

mayonnaise
celery salt
sugar

Combine pork, apple, and lemon juice. Add mayonnaise to moisten, and season with celery salt and sugar to taste. Serve well chilled in lettuce cups. Serves 4.

Cranberry Salad

1 lb. ground cranberries
1-1/2 c. sugar
No. 2 can crushed pineapple

1 pkg. miniature marshmallows
1 c. whipping cream

Grind cranberries, add sugar; let stand 2 hours. Add pineapple (do not drain) and marshmallows. Fold in whipped cream. Freeze. Cut in slices or squares to serve.

Lime Cream Fruit Mold

2 pkg. (3 oz.) lime Jello
1 c. boiling water
1 T. lime juice (optional)
2 c. sour cream

1 can (20-1/2 oz.) crushed pineapple with juice
1 c. quartered maraschino cherries, drained
1/2 c. pecans (chopped)

Dissolve gelatin in boiling water. Cool. Add lime juice. Beat in sour cream with wire whip. Add pineapple with juice. Chill until partly set. Fold in cherries and pecans. Turn into mold and chill until firm.

Cranberry Salad

1 c. ground cranberries
1 c. sugar
1 pkg. lemon gelatin
1 c. hot water

1 c. pineapple syrup
1 c. crushed pineapple (well drained)
1 c. celery (chopped)
1/2 c. walnuts (broken)

Combine cranberries and sugar. Dissolve gelatin in hot water, add syrup. Chill until partially set. Add cranberry mixture, pineapple, walnuts, and celery. Pour into oiled 9 x 9 x 1-3/4 inch pan. Chill until firm. Cut in squares. Serve on crisp lettuce with mayonnaise. Serves 6.

7-Up Salad

1 large pkg. lime gelatin
2 small pkg. cream cheese
2 c. 7-Up soda

1 pkg. Dream Whip (prepared)
1 small can crushed pineapple
Walnuts

Dissolve gelatin in 2 c. boiling water. Beat in cheese with rotary beater or electric mixer. Add 7-Up. Chill until partially set. Beat in Dream Whip, stir in pineapple and chopped nuts. Chill until firm. Lemon gelatin may be substituted for lime gelatin. Yield: about 12 servings.

The best cosmetic in the world is an active mind
that is always finding something new.

M.M. Atkeson

Red Raspberry Salad

1 (3 oz.) pkg. lemon gelatin
1 c. boiling water
8 oz. pkg. cream cheese
1 c. coffee cream
3 T. powdered sugar
1 t. vanilla

2 (3 oz.) raspberry gelatin
3 c. boiling water
2 pkg. frozen raspberries
   (drained well)
1 c. raspberry juice

Dissolve lemon gelatin in boiling water. Add softened cream cheese, powdered sugar, coffee cream and vanilla. Pour in oiled ring mold and allow to set. Dissolve raspberry gelatin in boiling water; add raspberries and juice. Pour on top of first mixture and allow to set.

Casseroles and Main Dishes

Hot Chicken Salad

2 c. chicken (cut-up, cooked)
2 c. celery (cut fine)
1 can cream of chicken soup
1 c. mayonnaise
Salt to taste

1 T. lemon juice
1 T. onion (chopped)
1 c. water chestnuts (sliced)
1 c. potato chips (crushed)

Combine all ingredients, except sprinkle crushed potato chips on top. Bake in 350° oven for 15 minutes or until slightly brown. Serves 6 to 8.

Spring Chicken Oriental

1 2-1/2 to 3 lb. fryer, cut up
1/4 c. butter
1 No. 2 can pineapple chunks
1/4 c. brown sugar
2 T. cornstarch
1/2 t. salt

1/3 c. vinegar
1 T. soy sauce
1 T. toasted sesame seed
1 (4 oz.) can sliced mushrooms
1/2 medium green pepper (thinly sliced)
1/2 medium onion (sliced)

Brown chicken slowly in butter, cover and cook for 20 minutes. Remove lid and cook 20 minutes longer. While chicken is browning, drain syrup from pineapple and measure out 1 cup. Heat syrup to boiling and stir in mixture of brown sugar, cornstarch, salt and vinegar. Stir constantly until sauce thickens. Add pineapple chunks and remaining ingredients and continue to simmer on low heat stirring occasionally to prevent sticking. Pour sauce over chicken, cook 5 minutes. Delicious served with fluffy steamed rice.

Grandmother's Hash

2 T. fat
1 medium onion, diced
2 c. leftover roast beef, diced
2 c. diced potatoes (cooked)

1 c. gravy (optional)
1 c. water
any vegetable (optional)

Lightly brown the onion in fat. Add all other ingredients and simmer slowly for 30 minutes until the flavors have blended and it is piping hot. Note: If gravy is omitted, use 2 cups water. Yield: 6 servings.

Potatoes Au Gratin

1/2 c. American cheese, grated
2 c. medium white sauce
4 medium potatoes, sliced

1/2 green pepper, chopped
1 c. buttered crumbs

Add cheese to warm white sauce, stirring until blended. Place alternate layers of potatoes, white sauce and peppers in a greased casserole. Top with crumbs. Bake covered for 20 minutes at 350°F; uncover and bake an additional 10 minutes. Yield: 6 servings.

Zucchini Supreme

6 small zucchini squash
1/2 c. diced onion
1 c. sliced mushrooms, fresh or canned

2 T. minced parsley
2/3 c. tomatoes (canned or fresh)
2/3 lb. sausage, crumbled

Wash squash and cut off ends. Do NOT peel. Cook in boiling water for 5 minutes. Halve lengthwise. Remove pulp with spoon. Save 1 cup pulp. Saute onion in skillet coated with corn oil. Add mushrooms, continue to saute until mushrooms are cooked. Add reserved pulp, parsley, tomato and sausage; cook 5 minutes. Fill zucchini shells and place in shallow baking dish. Cover and bake at 350° for 25 minutes. Uncover and bake 10 minutes longer.

*Always drive as if your children
were in the other car.*

Chicken Casserole

1 stewing chicken (3-1/2 lb. or larger)
1 c. celery (chopped)
1 c. nuts (chopped; walnuts, pecans or almonds)
2 T. onion (minced)
Fine buttered bread crumbs or crushed potato chips

1 can cream of chicken soup
1 c. mayonnaise
2 T. lemon juice
3/4 t. salt
1/4 t. pepper
Paprika

Steam chicken until tender. Remove meat from bones, cut into bite-sized pieces. Mix with remaining ingredients except crumbs and paprika. Turn into greased 2 qt. casserole, top with crumbs or chips, sprinkle with paprika. Bake uncovered at 350° for about 30 minutes or until bubbly. Casserole may be frozen before or after baking.

He-Man Spanish Rice

1 lb. ground beef
1/2 c. onion, chopped
1/4 c. green pepper, chopped
1 t. salt
1/8 t. chili powder

1/2 small clove garlic (minced)
1 can tomato soup
1 c. water
1 t. Worcestershire sauce
1/3 c. rice

Cook beef, onion, green pepper, salt, chili powder, and garlic in skillet until beef is browned and crumbly. Add remaining ingredients. Cover; cook 30 minutes or until rice is tender, stirring often. Yield: 3-4 servings.

Baked Meatballs

1 egg
1/4 c. milk
1-1/2 t. onion (minced)
1-1/2 slices bread (cubed)

1 t. salt
1/8 t. pepper
1 lb. ground beef

Heat oven to 350°. Beat egg and milk. Stir in onion, bread, and seasonings. Add beef and mix well. Shape into balls, using mixture for each ball. Place in shallow pan. Bake 30 to 40 minutes. Makes about 7 meatballs.

Simple Hot Dish

2 lb. hamburger
1 medium onion,
  chopped and browned
1 pkg. macaroni (cooked)

2 No. 2 cans cream style corn
2 cans chicken-rice soup
2 t. salt

Combine all ingredients and place in a casserole and bake 1-1/2 hours at 350°.

Meat Loaf with Vegetables

2 lb. ground beef
1 can vegetable soup
1 egg (beaten)
1/2 c. bread crumbs
1 onion (chopped)

1 T. Worcestershire sauce
1 T. prepared mustard
1 t. salt
1/4 t. black pepper

Mix above and shape the mixture into a loaf. Bake about 1 hour at 350°.

Baked Soup Casserole

hamburger (soup or stew meat)
onion
potatoes
cabbage

carrots
celery
salt and pepper
canned tomatoes or tomato juice

Put meat and vegetables in layers in casserole or roaster. Top with canned tomatoes or tomato juice and bake 1-1/2 to 2 hours at 375°.

Baked Pork Chops

6 thick pork chops
salt and pepper
apple juice
1 (20 oz.) can pie sliced apples

1/2 t. cinnamon
1/4 t. nutmeg
1/8 t. ground cloves

Brown chops on both sides in their own fat. Place in flat baking dish, sprinkle with salt and pepper. Add enough apple juice to cover chops, cover pan. Bake at 350° for 1 hour. Top with drained apple slices, sprinkle with spices. Return to oven, uncovered. Bake 20 minutes at 350°.

Mock Chop Suey

MIX:

1 can mushroom soup
1 can cream of chicken soup
1 can chicken noodle soup
1 can peas and liquid
1 small can mushrooms and liquid
1 can bean sprouts
1 small can water chestnuts
   (optional)

1 small can pimiento
1 c. water
1 c. raw rice
1 c. celery (diced)
1 lb. hamburger
1 c. chicken or turkey (diced, cooked)
2 T. soy sauce
1 onion

Saute hamburger with onion. Add to other ingredients and bake at 350° for 1-1/2 hours.

Fu Man Chew

2 T. oil
1 c. onions (chopped)
1 c. celery (sliced)
2 lb. ground beef
2 cans cream of mushroom soup
   (undiluted)
1 c. uncooked rice

1 can bean sprouts with liquid
1 flat can water chestnuts
   (drained and sliced)
4 T. soy sauce
Salt and pepper
1 can chow mein noodles
1 pkg. frozen pea pods

Saute onion and celery in oil for 5 minutes. Add ground beef; when beef is brown add soup, rice, bean sprouts, chestnuts, soy sauce, seasonings. Pour into large casserole and bake, covered for 30 minutes at 350°. Then add pea pods, which have been slightly thawed and top casserole with noodles. Bake uncovered for 30 minutes at 350°.

Chop Suey Hotdish

1 c. rice (uncooked)
1-1/2 lb. ground beef
1 can chop suey vegetables

1 can mushroom soup with 1/2 can water
1 medium onion (chopped)

Brown meat, onion. Season with salt, pepper, and poultry seasoning. Alternate layers of rice, meat and vegetables in baking dish. Add a little soy sauce, cover with soup and water mixture. Bake 1-1/4 hours at 350°. Cover dish for baking. If cooked rice is used, reduce baking time.

Baked Chicken Casserole

1 cup up fryer, sprinkled with pepper. Add a few red pepper flakes. Sprinkle with toasted slivered almonds. Mix 1/2 can each of cream of mushroom and cream of chicken soup with 1/4 c. dry wine. Pour over chicken. Sprinkle with more slivered almonds and Parmesan cheese. Bake in 350° oven for 1-1/2 hours. Serve with noodles or rice.

Chicken and Stuffing Pie

CRUST

1 8-oz. pkg. herb-seasoned
   stuffing mix
3/4 c. chicken broth

1/2 c. butter (melted)
1 egg (beaten)

Mix together all ingredients. Press into a greased 10 inch pie plate.

FILLING

1 4-oz. can mushrooms
2 t. flour
1/2 c. onion (chopped)
1 T. butter
1 (10-1/2 oz.) can chicken
   giblet gravy
3 c. chicken (cooked, cubed)

1 c. peas
2 T. pimientos (diced)
1 T. parsley flakes
1 t. Worcestershire sauce
1/2 t. thyme
4 slices American cheese

Drain mushrooms, combine mushroom liquid with flour; set aside. Saute mushrooms and onion in melted butter. Stir in all ingredients except cheese. Heat thoroughly. Turn into crust. Bake 375° for 20 minutes. Cut each cheese slice into 4 strips. Place in lattice design on pie. Bake 5 more minutes. Note: For moist crust use more chicken broth.

Chicken in Cream

1 or 2 fryer chickens
flour
salt

pepper
butter or oleo
1 qt. cream

Cut chickens in pieces; wash in cold water; drain; roll in flour. Fry until brown on all sides in butter or oleo, put in roaster with salt and pepper to taste, and add cream. Bake 375° for 1 hour.

Oven Chow Mein Casserole

1/2 lb. ground beef
1/2 lb. pork sausage
2 T. butter
2 c. onions (chopped)
1 c. rice (uncooked)

2 c. hot water
1 can cream of mushroom soup
1/2 t. salt
1/4 t. pepper
1/3 c. soy sauce

Put meat and sausage in pan and brown lightly in butter. Add remaining ingredients. Pour into 2 qt. casserole and cover. Bake in 350° oven for 1 hour. Stir occasionally.

Chicken Tremendous

1 c. uncooked rice
1 pkg. dry onion soup mix
1 fryer chicken (cut up)

1 can cream of chicken or
    mushroom soup (diluted)
salt and pepper to taste

Place rice in greased casserole, add cut chicken pieces; sprinkle with dry soup mix, seasonings. Pour diluted soup over all. Cover. Bake at 350° for 1 to 1-1/2 hours, or longer if preferred.

Round Steak

round steak
2 T. shortening
1 bottle Russian dressing

1 pkg. dry onion soup mix
1/2 c. water

Brown a round steak in shortening. Mix remaining ingredients, pour over meat and simmer 1 hour.

Onion-Beef Macaroni Casserole

1-1/2 lb. ground beef
1 envelope onion soup mix
1 T. flour
1 can tomato sauce (8 oz.)

2 c. water
2 c. cooked macaroni (drained)
1/4 c. cheddar cheese (grated)

Brown meat well; drain off excess fat. Stir in onion soup mix, flour, tomato sauce and water. Simmer, covered, for 5 minutes. Stir in macaroni. Turn into 1-1/2 qt. casserole. Sprinkle with cheese. Bake 15 minutes at 400°. Serves 6.

Peanut Burger Casserole

8 oz. pkg. shell macaroni
2 c. onion (chopped)
1/2 c. green pepper (chopped)
2 T. salad oil
2 lb. ground beef
2 t. salt

1/4 t. pepper
1 can cream of mushroom soup
1 c. evaporated milk
1 c. shredded cheddar cheese
2 T. Worcestershire sauce
1 c. peanuts (coarsely chopped)

Cook macaroni according to directions until barely tender, drain well.

In large kettle combine onion, green pepper, oil and meat. Cook over medium heat until meat has browned, breaking meat into chunks as it cooks, season with salt and pepper.

Stir in soup, evaporated milk, 2/3 c. cheese, and Worcestershire sauce. Add macaroni, cover and simmer 20 minutes, stirring occasionally. Turn into 2-1/2 qt. buttered casserole, sprinkle with remaining cheese and chopped peanuts. Bake at 350° for 30 minutes. Serves 10.

Lasagna

SIMMER 1/2 HOUR:
1-1/2 lb. ground chuck
2 cloves garlic (minced)
2 T. oil
1 pkg. onion soup

1 c. tomato paste
water to rinse can
2 t. oregano

salt and pepper to taste
1 carton cream cottage cheese
parmesan cheese for topping

1 8-oz. pkg. mozzarella cheese
lasagna noodles

Saute garlic in oil, add meat and brown. Add rest of ingredients. Simmer 1/2 hour. Cook noodles 15 minutes in boiling salted water. Rinse. Grease pan. Place layer of noodles, meat mixture, cottage cheese and mozzarella. Repeat until all is used. Sprinkle with parmesan cheese. Bake until brown on top.

Pearled Barley Hot Dish

1 c. barley soaked overnight, then boiled 1/2 hour

BROWN IN PAN:
1 lb. ground beef
1 onion (chopped)

1 c. celery

ADD:
1 c. tomato soup
1 c. mushroom soup

1 c. frozen vegetables (undrained)
Salt and pepper

Mix and bake 1 hour at 350°.

Baked Bean Casserole

8 slices of bacon
1/2 c. brown sugar
1 t. dry mustard
1 t. salt
1/2 c. cider vinegar

2 large onions
1 c. red beans
1 c. lima beans
1 large can pork and beans
1 large can butter beans

Cut up bacon and fry. Add brown sugar, dry mustard, salt and vinegar. Cut onions in rings and cook with the above mixture until onions are tender. Put into a casserole (large) and add all the remaining beans. Bake at 350° for 1 hour.

Barbecued Spareribs

3 to 4 lb. ribs (cut in pieces)
1 lemon
1 large onion
1 c. catsup
1/3 c. Worcestershire sauce

1 t. chili powder
1 t. salt
2 dashes Tabasco sauce
2 c. water

Place ribs in shallow roasting pan, meaty side up; on each piece, place a slice of unpeeled lemon and a thin slice of onion. Roast in a very hot oven 450° for 30 minutes. Combine remaining ingredients, bring to a boil and pour over ribs. Continue baking in moderate oven 350° until tender, about 45 minutes to 1 hour. Baste ribs with the sauce every 15 minutes; if sauce gets too thick, add more water. Makes 4 servings.

Hamburger Noodle Casserole

1 lb. hamburger
1 medium onion (chopped)
1 can tomato soup

1 can whole kernel corn
1/2 pkg. egg noodles
Lawry's salt

Brown hamburger and onion in skillet , season to taste. . Add tomato soup and corn. Add egg noodles (cooked beforehand). To thin, add catsup and water if desired.

Chicken and Noodle Casserole

4 oz. noodles
1 qt. water
1 T. salt
3 T. fat
3 T. flour
1/4 t. paprika

1 t. salt
1 c. chicken stock
1 c. milk
1/4 c. black olives (chopped)
2 c. chicken (cubed, cooked)
1 T. lemon juice

Boil noodles in 1 qt. boiling water with 1 T. salt. Drain if needed. While noodles are cooking, melt fat. Mix flour, salt and paprika with fat to make a smooth paste. Slowly add chicken stock and milk. Add olives, cubed chicken and lemon juice. Combine with noodles and pour into 1-1/2 qt. casserole. Cover and bake in 350° oven for 45 minutes. Serve hot. (To store: cool, package and freeze).

Baked Macaroni and Cheese

8-9 oz. macaroni
3 c. white sauce
3/4 c. cheddar or sharp cheese

1 T. onion (chopped)
1/2 t. dry mustard
1/2 to 1 t. Worcestershire sauce

Cook macaroni as directed on package. Make white sauce, then add other ingredients gradually. Alternate macaroni and sauce in casserole. Sprinkle top with wheat germ. Bake in 350° oven or 375° for 25 minutes.

WHITE SAUCE

Melt 3 T. butter in top of double boiler or saucepan. Shake 3 T. flour with 1 c. milk in a jar. Pour in with butter, then add remaining 2 C. of milk, plus 1 t. salt and 1/4 t. pepper.

Veal or Pork Casserole

1 lb. veal or pork steak
3 T. flour
2 T. fat
1-1/2 c. celery (cut up)
2 small onions (chopped)

1 can cream of chicken soup
1 can cream of mushroom soup
1 can water
2 T. soy sauce
1/2 c. dry rice

Cut meat into small cubes, flour, and brown in fat. Add remaining ingredients and bake in 325° oven for 2-1/2 hours. Don't add salt.

Baked Chop Suey

1 lb. pork and 1 lb. veal steak
1 lb. beef round steak
1 c. onion (chopped)
1 c. celery (chopped)
salt and pepper
Celery and green pepper
  (optional)

1 can cream of chicken soup
1 can cream of mushroom soup
1/4 c. soy sauce
1 c. raw rice (washed in boiling water)
1 can bean sprouts
1 can chop suey vegetables

Cut meat in small pieces, brown with onion and cook until tender. Add a little water and cook with celery and green pepper. Season to taste. Add soups, 2 cans water and soy sauce. Add 1/2 cup water and rice. Add bean sprouts and chop suey vegetables. Stir well every once in a while during baking. Bake 1-1/2 hours at 350°. Add a little water if it seems too thick. Serve with chow mein noodles. Serves 12.

Cheese Oriental

6 c. hot cooked rice (2 c. raw)
2 c. shredded cheddar cheese
1-1/2 c. milk
3/4 t. salt
2 T. butter

1/2 c. green pepper (chopped)
1 c. celery (chopped)
1/4 c. pimientos (chopped)
3 hard cooked eggs
3 T. flour

Cook rice according to directions. Combine cheese, milk, and salt in top of double boiler over water, stirring occasionally until well blended. Melt butter in skillet, add green pepper, celery, and onion; cook until tender. Add flour to vegetable mixture and blend thoroughly. Add vegetables, pimiento and chopped eggs to cheese sauce. Pack hot fluffy rice into 1-1/2 qt. buttered ring mold, unmold rice on large heated platter, fill ring with cheese mixture.

American Chop Suey

1-1/2 lb. ground beef
1 onion (chopped)
1 c. celery (chopped)
1/2 c. regular rice

1 can cream of mushroom soup
1 can cream of chicken soup
2 cans water
1/4 c. soy sauce

Brown meat and onions. Mix all ingredients. Bake 1/2 hour at 375°. Stir so rice won't be on the bottom. Bake 1 hour longer. Serve with chow mein noodles.

Round Steak Casserole

1-1/2 lb. round steak,
   cut in 1/2" pieces
3 T. butter or margarine
1 medium onion, chopped
6 small potatoes, sliced

3 carrots, sliced (optional)
salt and pepper to taste
Dash of garlic salt
2 c. beef bouillon

Brown steak in butter; remove from pan. Saute onion in drippings until lightly browned. In a shallow baking dish, layer half of meat, onion, potatoes and carrots. Season with salt, pepper and garlic salt. Repeat layers. Pour bouillon over all. Bake covered at 300°F. for 2 hours. Add more bouillon if necessary. Yield: 4-6 servings.

Big Burger

2 c. flour
2 c. mashed potato flakes
1/2 c. butter
3/4 c. milk
1 lb. hamburger
1 pkg. Sloppy Joe seasoning mix

16 oz. tomato sauce
1 c. (4 oz.) mozzarella cheese
Milk
2 T. butter (melted)
1/2 c. mashed potato flakes

In large bowl combine flour, flakes; cut in butter. Stir in milk with fork. Dough will be stiff. Pat half of dough in 10 inch pie pan. Brown hamburger, add seasoning mix and tomato sauce. Pour over dough. Sprinkle shredded cheese on top. Add rest of dough on top. Brush with milk. Sprinkle top with mixture of butter and 1/2 c. flakes. Bake at 425° for 20-25 minutes until brown.

Pasties (*Ingredients for 1 pasty*)

1/2 lb. pork and beef (cut in
    small pieces)
1/4 c. onions (diced fine)
1/2. c. potatoes (sliced fine
    or cubed)

1/4 c. carrots or rutabaga
    (sliced or cubed)
Salt and pepper (to taste)
Butter
Pastry

All ingredients for pasty are raw to begin. You may also use ground beef instead of the beef and pork cut small, and you may wish to use less meat and more potatoes and vegetables.

Roll out pastry into circles (using 8 inch pan for guide). Place filling on crust and dot with butter (if meat is lean) and bring up edges of crust to meet over the mixture on top, crimp edges of crust together to seal. Bake 1 hour at 400°. One secret to a delicious pasty is not to eat it immediately after baking but leave in oven (slightly cooled oven) for at least half an hour after baking, or remove pasties from oven to racks immediately after baking and cover with towel and let rest for about half an hour or until cool enough to eat. Serve plain or pass catsup.

Macaroni Loaf Souffle

1 c. macaroni (raw)
1 c. cream
1 c. soft bread crumbs
1 c. cheese (grated)
3 eggs (separated)

1/2 c. butter
2 pimientos (cut up)
1 T. onion (chopped)
1 green pepper (chopped)

Boil macaroni. Separate eggs, beat yolks and combine with other ingredients. Fold in beaten whites. Bake 350° 1-1/2 hours in buttered tin in pan of hot water. Serve with mushroom sauce.

Mystery Casserole

1 lb. ground beef
2 c. celery
1 can chicken-rice soup

1 can vegetable soup
1 can mushrooms
1 can Chinese noodles

Brown ground beef, put in casserole. Add rest of ingredients. Use half can Chinese noodles. Bake 1/2 hour at 350°. Add rest of noodles on top and bake for another 1/2 hour.

Undercover Meatballs

1 lb. ground beef
1 egg
1/2 c. salted cashews

1 t. seasoned salt
1 t. onion (minced)
1 can refrigerator biscuits

Combine first 5 ingredients and shape into balls. Separate biscuits and roll out into circles. Place meatballs on cookie sheet and cover each with flattened biscuit, pressing edge down to touch pan. Bake at 400° for 20-25 minutes.

Sausage and Lentil Casserole

1 pkg. lentils
2 T. cooking oil
2 medium onions (chopped)
3 garlic cloves (crushed)
1 can tomatoes (drained)

2 lb. Polish sausage
1 t. sugar
1/2 t. pepper
1 bay leaf
Salt (to taste)

Cook lentils in large saucepan for 20 minutes or until tender but not mushy. Drain and reserve liquid. Heat oil in flameproof casserole. Stir in onions and garlic. Cook until tender. Chop tomatoes and add to onions and garlic. Cook until liquid has evaporated. Peel casings from sausage and cut into 1/2 inch slices. Toss sausage with tomato mixture and add lentils, sugar, pepper, bay leaf and salt. Stir in a little of the lentil liquid and bake at 350° about 30 minutes. Add more liquid if dry.

Sausage Squash

3 acorn squash
1 lb. bulk pork sausage
3/4 c. celery (chopped)
1/3 c. onion (chopped)

1/4 c. green pepper (chopped)
1/2 c. parmesan cheese (grated)
3 T. dairy sour cream

Halve and seed squash. Sprinkle insides with salt and pepper and place cut side down in shallow baking pan, bake at 375° until squash is tender. To test for doneness, pierce squash with long tonged fork. While squash bakes, cook sausage; when meat starts to brown, add celery, onion, and green pepper; cook until meat is thoroughly done. Drain off fat. Reserve about 2 T. parmesan; stir rest of parmesan into sausage. Stir in sour cream. Add salt and pepper to taste.

Turn squash cut side up and fill cavities with sausage mixture, sprinkle with reserved parmesan. Bake 15 minutes. Makes 6 servings.

Cabbage Rolls

1/2 c. cooked rice
1 c. milk
1-1/4 lb. ground beef
2 t. salt

1/4 t. pepper
1 small onion (chopped)
2 T. brown sugar
1/2 c. hot water

Mix together rice, milk, ground beef, salt, pepper, and onion. Roll in steamed cabbage leaves and place in baking dish. Mix brown sugar and water and sprinkle over rolls. Cover and bake at 350° for about 1 hour.

Pork Chop and Potato Scallop

4 pork chops
1 can cream of mushroom soup
1/2 c. sour cream
1/4 c. water

2 T. parsley, chopped
4 c. potatoes, thinly sliced
salt and pepper to taste

Brown chops. Blend soup, sour cream, water and parsley. In a 2 quart casserole alternate layers of potatoes sprinkled with salt and pepper and sauce. Top with chops. Cover and bake at 375° for 1 hour and 15 minutes. Yield: 4 servings.

Beef Stroganoff

3 lb. stew meat (cut in 3/4 inch
   pieces and dipped in flour)
1-1/2 c. onion (chopped)
1 clove garlic (2 if you
   really like garlic)
1 6-oz. can mushrooms w/liquid

3 c. sour cream
3 cans tomato soup
2 T. Worcestershire sauce
6 drops Tabasco sauce
1-1/2 t. salt
1/8 t. pepper

Brown meat (coated with flour) in 6 T. hot fat. Add all the other ingredients and stir often while simmering. Cook until tender, about 2 or 3 hours. This requires very low heat. Serve over mashed potatoes, noodles or spaghetti.

*Sometimes one pays most for the
things one gets for nothing.*

Pork Chops and Stuffing

4 pork chops
3 c. bread cubes
2 T. onion (chopped)
1 can cream of mushroom soup

1/4 c. butter (melted)
1/4 c. water
1/4 t. poultry seasoning

Brown 4 pork chops on both sides, pour off drippings. Lightly mix bread, onion, butter, water and seasoning. Place a mound of stuffing on each chop. Blend mushroom soup with 1/3 c. water, pour over. Bake at 350° about 1 hour. 4 servings.

Potato Sausage

1-1/2 lb. lean ground beef
1/2 lb. lean ground pork
2 lb. potatoes
1 onion

3 T. salt
1/2 t. pepper
1/4 c. beef broth
1/4 lb. casings (dry, salted)

Soak casing in water to remove salt. Rinse thoroughly. Grind potatoes and onion. Mix together with seasonings, broth and ground meat. Stuff into casings. Boil slowly in salted water for 1 hour to cook.

Ham Loaf with Glaze

1-1/2 lb. ham
1-1/4 lb. pork
2 eggs

1-1/2 c. bread crumbs
1/2 c. onion (chopped)
1/2 c. milk

Grind pork and ham. Combine with other ingredients and press into ring mold or loaf pan. Bake 1-1/4 hours at 350°.

GLAZE

1/2 c. brown sugar
1 T. mustard

1 T. vinegar
1 T. water

Combine. Use to baste ham loaf the last 30 minutes of baking.

Opportunities are seldom labeled.

Speedy Spaghetti

1-1/2 lb. ground beef
8 oz. pkg. dry spaghetti

1 large can tomato soup
1 can Spanish rice

Cook spaghetti until soft. Sprinkle salt in bottom of frying pan, then break ground beef into small pieces. Fry on both sides. After spaghetti is cooked, drain off water, add ground beef, can of tomato soup, can of Spanish rice and mix well. Makes 6-8 servings.

Meat and Tater Pie

Make pastry for a two crust pie.

COMBINE:

1 lb. ground beef
1/2 c. milk
1/2 envelope dry onion soup
Dash of pepper

Dash of allspice
1 12-oz. pkg. hash brown
    potatoes (frozen)

Line pie tin with pastry. Combine meat, milk, soup mix, pepper and allspice. Pat into the crust. Spread potatoes on top. Put on top crust. Bake 1 hour at 350°.

Meat Pie

1 lb. hamburger
1 can tomato soup

1/2 c. onion (chopped)
1/2 c. celery (chopped)

Simmer 20 minutes. Bake 20 minutes.

2 c. flour
5 T. butter
3 t. baking powder

1 t. paprika
3/4 c. milk

Mix. Drop by spoon on the meat pie. Bake.

Chance makes our parents, but choice
makes our friends.

New Year's Meat Pie

5 lb. ground pork
2 T. cinnamon
1 level T. cloves
1 c. mashed potatoes
Pastry

4 slices bread (crumbled)
3-1/2 T. salt
1 t. pepper
3 large onions

Combine all filling ingredients and divide into pastry filled tins. Cover with top crust and bake in moderately hot oven. Very rich.

Corned Beef Casserole

8 oz. medium noodles,
    cooked & drained
1 (12 oz.) can corned beef
    (broken into small pieces)

1-1/4 c. milk
1 can cream of mushroom soup
1/4 c. onion (chopped)
1/3 lb. Velveeta cheese, cubed

Mix the milk and soup together until well blended. Then mix with rest of ingredients. Cover with buttered cracker crumbs. Bake 1 hour at 350° (bake covered first 40 minutes, then uncovered last 20 minutes to brown). Serves 6.

Pizza Crust *(Makes 2 large pizzas)*

1 pkg. dry yeast
3 C. flour
2 T. soft shortening

1 c. warm water
1-1/2 t. salt

Add yeast to the warm water in a medium sized bowl. Let stand a few minutes, then stir to dissolve. Mix half the flour with the salt and soft shortening. Beat until smooth, then mix in remaining flour a little at a time until it disappears. Beat hard. Remove from the bowl to a lightly floured board. Cover and let rest 5 to 10 minutes. Preheat oven to 400°. Divide in two. Dip finger in oil and pat out each half of dough onto a greased baking sheet, making 11 inch rounds. Keep outside edges a little thicker than the center. Add filling of your choice. Bake pizzas 20 to 30 minutes. Note: The baked pizza may be frozen after it is cooled. Wrap in foil. Reheat for serving in the foil.

Pork and Beef Pie *(4 Pies)*

4 lb. ground pork
1 lb. ground beef
Salt, cloves, allspice, and pepper to taste

4 large onions (ground)
4 potatoes (ground)

Cook slowly all ingredients in 2 qts. of water. Cool. Use for filling in double crust pies.

Pizzaburger Pie

1 lb. ground beef
1/2 c. evaporated milk
1/2 c. pizza sauce
1/3 c. fine dry bread crumbs
1/4 c. onion (chopped)
3/4 t. salt

1/2 t. dried oregano (crushed)
1/8 t. pepper
1 (8 inch) unbaked pastry shell
1 c. shredded cheese
1 t. Worcestershire sauce

Combine first 8 ingredients. Spread in unbaked pastry shell. Bake at 350° for 35 to 40 minutes. Toss together cheese and Worcestershire sauce; spread atop meat. Bake 10 minutes more. Remove from oven; let stand 10 minutes before serving.

Favorite Casserole

1 lb. hamburger
1/2 c. onion (chopped)
1/2 c. celery (chopped)
1/4 c. green pepper
1 T. shortening
3/4 c. processed cheese (diced)

1 can cream of chicken soup
1-1/4 c. milk
1-1/2 c. cooked rice
1 t. salt
Pepper (to taste)
Crumbs for topping

Melt shortening in skillet. Combine hamburger, onion, celery, green pepper, salt and pepper. Cook in fat stirring often until meat is lightly browned. Combine soup, milk, and rice in saucepan; bring to a boil. Remove from heat and add cheese, stirring well. Place meat mixture in casserole. Stir in soup mixture, top with crumbs. Bake at 375° for 30 minutes.

It's just as easy to look for the good things in life
rather than the bad.

Poor Man's Dish

1-1/2 lb. hamburger
6 T. milk
1/4 lb. butter or margarine
1 onion (chopped)
1/4 t. sage 1/2 loaf bread

1/4 t. oregano
2 cans cream of celery soup
1 can cream of chicken soup
1/2 can water

Put hamburger in baking pan, sprinkle with milk. Melt butter or margarine in frying pan, add onion, sage and oregano. Pour over meat. Dice bread and put on top of hamburger. Mix soups and water, pour over top of bread and bake 1-1/2 hours at 350°.

Beef Stroganoff

1-1/2 lbs. beef cut in strips
    or tenderloin tips

1 T. butter

Brown meat lightly. Add to beef:

3/4 T. onion (grated)
2 T. butter (browned)

3/4 c. mushrooms

ADD:
Salt
Pepper
1 c. sour cream

Little nutmeg
1/2 t. basil

Heat but do not boil. Stir sour cream in last. 4 servings.

Hamburger Onion Pie

1 c. Bisquick
1/3 c. cream
1 lb. hamburger
1/2 can onion soup

2 eggs (beaten)
1 c. cottage cheese
paprika

Combine Bisquick and cream, stir with fork, roll out to fit 9 inch pan. Brown hamburger, add onion soup. Mix 2 eggs with cottage cheese, combine with meat mixture. Pour into unbaked shell, sprinkle with paprika. Bake at 375° for 30 minutes.

Beef Stroganoff

2 lb. sirloin steak
1 small can sliced mushrooms
1 can chicken broth
1 small onion (chopped)

2/3 c. cooking sherry or
  1 T. vinegar
3 T. sour cream
White rice or egg noodles for 4

Cut sirloin into 2 inch squares. Brown lightly on both sides, in bacon grease. Add mushrooms, chicken broth and onion. Cover and simmer for 2 hours on low heat. 15 minutes before end of cooking time add sherry or vinegar, stir, cover for 15 minutes more. In the meantime cook rice or egg noodles to serve 4. Remove meat from heat and stir in sour cream. Serve immediately over cooked rice or noodles.

Beef Stroganoff

3 cube steaks (cut in strips)
1 medium onion (chopped)
1 clove garlic (sliced)
1/2 pt. sour cream
1 can cream of mushroom soup

1 T. catsup
1 T. Worcestershire sauce
1 4-oz. can of mushrooms
  (do not drain)

Brown cut up steak strips, onions and garlic in skillet. Mix sour cream, soup, catsup, sauce, and mushrooms. Stir mixture into the browned meat. Heat through but do not boil. Serve over cooked noodles or hot rice.

Curried Rice With Chicken

3-3-1/2 lb. whole fryer
1/2 c. raw rice (Uncle Ben's)
1/4 c. margarine
1 stalk celery (chopped)
1 medium onion (chopped)

About 2 t. curry powder
1 can cream of mushroom soup
2 T. butter
salt, pepper, paprika
1 t. parsley (chopped)

Cook rice according to package directions. Meanwhile, saute celery and onion with parsley and curry powder in margarine. Add half a can of mushroom soup and mix well, add cooked rice. Stuff the chicken with the rice mix. Melt butter and pour over stuffed chicken. Sprinkle with salt, pepper and paprika. Cover loosely and cook for 2 hours and 15 minutes at 325°. Cook uncovered for 45 minutes more or until browned. Add curry powder to taste to the leftover mushroom soup, heat and serve as gravy.

Washday Hot Dish

1 lb. hamburger	2 c. tomatoes
1 medium onion (chopped)	3 c. raw potatoes (diced)
1/2 c. raw rice	1 can red kidney beans
1 c. celery (diced)	Salt and pepper

Brown hamburger and onions. Pour in bottom of casserole. Cover with layers of rice, celery, potatoes and kidney beans. Pour tomatoes over top and bake at 350° for 1 hour or until potatoes are done.

Oven Beef Stew

2 lb. stew meat	2 t. sugar
6 carrots	2 t. salt
3 medium onions	pepper
1 stalk celery	1/2 c. tomato juice
2 T. tapioca	

Cut meat, carrots, onions and celery in chunks. Place in bottom of casserole. Mix tapioca, sugar, salt, and pepper and sprinkle on. Pour tomato juice over all. Cover and bake 4 hours at 250°. Serve with cooked rice or mashed potatoes.

Bulgarian Rice

BROWN IN MAZOLA AND COOK UNTIL SOFT:

1 or 2 stalks celery (chopped fine)   1 large onion (chopped fine)

Add 1 c. raw rice and mix well (Uncle Ben's white rice works best). Put rice in long shallow pan and pour 3 cups rich chicken broth over it and mix well. Add 1 t. salt, 1/2 t. pepper and mix well. Fresh chopped parsley may also be added. Cook at 350° about 1 hour or until rice is cooked and all broth absorbed.

Skillet Casserole

1 c. elbow spaghetti or macaroni	1 can condensed chili-beef soup
1 lb. ground beef	3 slices American cheese (sharp)
1 can condensed tomato soup	

Brown beef, add soups and cooked spaghetti or macaroni. Heat thoroughly. Place cheese slices on top of mixture. Cover 5 minutes until cheese is melted.

Five Hour Beef Stew *(Oven Stew)*

2 lb. stew meat (beef)	1 T. sugar
1 large can whole tomatoes	1/8 t. pepper
6 carrots (thickly sliced)	3 T. tapioca
3 onions (quartered)	potatoes (optional)
1 c. celery (sliced)	1/2 c. bread crumbs (optional)
1 T. salt	

Mix first 9 ingredients in large casserole, or Dutch oven. Cover tightly with lid or foil. Bake for 5 hours in 250° oven. Bread crumbs (and/or peeled potatoes) may be added 2 hours before stew is ready. Very good reheated.

Russian Fluff

1-1/2 lb. ground beef	1 onion (chopped)
1/2 green pepper (cut in pieces)	

Fry until brown. Then add and mix:

1 can corn (not drained)	1/2 c. uncooked rice
1 can mushrooms	1 can tomato soup

Bake 1 hour at 350° in covered casserole.

Italian Spaghetti

DICE FINE:

1 green pepper	1 clove garlic
1 medium onion	

1/4 c. Mazola oil	1 large can tomatoes
1-1/2 lb. ground beef	2 small cans water
2 cans tomato paste	spaghetti

Brown green pepper, onion and garlic in Mazola oil. Add ground beef and brown. Add tomato paste, tomatoes and water. Simmer 2 hours. Serve with boiled spaghetti and grated cheese.

With two eyes and one tongue you should see
twice as much as you say.

Tacos

1 lb. ground beef
1 can chili beans
1 small onion (chopped)
1/2 t. salt
1 pkg. tacos

1 c. lettuce (chopped)
1 c. tomato (chopped)
1 onion (chopped)
1 c. shredded cheese

Put into blender until smooth, beans and small onion. Brown meat and add salt and bean mixture. Fry tacos in a little hot oil and fold over. Fill taco shell with meat mixture and sprinkle with lettuce, tomatoes, onion, and cheese.

Tasty Casserole Supper

1 lb. ground beef
2 onions
1 c. tomato soup
1 c. green string beans

1/4 green pepper
potatoes
1 egg white

Brown the meat, season, add onions, soup, beans and green pepper. Place in a casserole and cover. Bake in a slow oven 1-1/2 hours. Cook potatoes, mash light and add 1 beaten egg white and a little cream and butter. Beat until fluffy and put on top of the meat dish and brown in the oven.

Hungarian Short Ribs

4 lb. short ribs
2 T. oil
2 medium onions
1-15-oz. can tomato sauce
1 c. water
1/4 c. brown sugar

1/4 c. vinegar
1 t. dry mustard
1 t. Worcestershire sauce
4-1/2 c. uncooked noodles
1 c. water
salt (to taste)

Brown meat in Dutch oven in the oil. Add onions. Blend tomato sauce and 1 c. water, brown sugar, vinegar, salt, mustard, and sauce. Pour over the meat. Cover and simmer 2 to 2-1/2 hours until meat is tender. Skim off fat. Stir in noodles and other cup of water. Cover and cook 15 minutes.

Easy Beef and Bean Casserole

1-1/2 lb. ground beef
1 large onion

1 c. catsup
2 (No. 303) cans pork and beans

Brown hamburger and onion. Combine with beans and catsup. Pour into baking dish. Bake at 375° for about 30 minutes.

Mixed Vegetable Casserole

2 lb. hamburger
2 pkg. frozen mixed vegetables
   (cooked)
1 can mushroom soup

1 onion
1/2 c. celery (chopped; optional)
1/4 c. green pepper (chopped; optional)
Potatoes (cooked and mashed)

Brown onion, celery and green pepper with hamburger. Add to cooked mixed vegetables and mushroom soup. Cover with mashed potatoes and bake 350° for 30 minutes.

Beef Kebab

3/4 c. vinegar
3/4 c. water
2 bay leaves
1 t. salt
1 t. sugar

1-1/2 lb. lean beef (top round)
   cut in 1 inch cubes
3 tomatoes (cut in sixths)
18 small mushrooms
6 slices bacon (cut in thirds)

Combine first 5 ingredients. Bring to a boil, simmer 5 minutes, and cool. Pour over beef cubes in large bowl; marinate 24 hours. Drain, save marinade. Arrange beef cubes, tomato wedges, mushrooms and bacon slices alternately on 6 skewers. Broil 15 minutes 3 to 4 inches from heat in shallow pan, turn often and baste with marinade. Makes 6 servings.

Hamburger Roll-Ups

1 lb. ground chuck
1 c. fine bread crumbs
1 T. lemon juice

1/4 c. cheddar cheese (finely grated)
1 t. salt

Combine all ingredients. Divide chuck into 6 pieces; shaping each into a roll 4 x 1-1/2 inches. Wrap each in a bacon slice. Lay on a broiler rack over a broiler pan. Bake 30 minutes in a 400° oven.

Old-Fashioned Corn Pudding

2 T. sugar
1-1/2 T. cornstarch
1 c. milk
3 eggs (beaten)

1 can (1 lb.) cream style corn
2 T. butter or margarine (melted)
1/2 t. salt
Dash nutmeg

Mix together sugar and cornstarch. Gradually add milk, stirring until smooth. Add eggs, corn, butter, and salt; mix well. Turn into a greased 1 qt. baking dish. Sprinkle with nutmeg. Place baking dish in pan of hot water. Bake at 300° for 1-3/4 hours or until custard is set. Yield: 4-6 portions.

Meat Loaf Supreme

2 lb. hamburger
2 eggs
1/4 c. onions (diced)
3/4 c. oatmeal

2 beef bouillon cubes in 1/2 c. boiling water
2 t. salt
1/2 c. shredded cheese
1 can beef vegetable soup (undiluted)

Mix all ingredients except the cheese. Place in baking pan and bake 1-1/4 hours at 375°. Remove from oven and sprinkle cheese on top. Return to oven. Bake 15 minutes more.

Country-Style Skillet Dinner

1 lb. ground chuck
2 T. margarine
2 c. medium size noodles
2 (8 oz.) can tomato sauce
1 (4 oz.) can mushrooms
1 t. salt

1 t. sugar
1/4 t. pepper
1/4 lb. natural Swiss cheese
    (shredded; about 1 c.)
1/4 c. parsley (chopped)

About 40 minutes before serving, in medium skillet over high heat, cook meat in hot margarine until browned. Stir in uncooked noodles, tomato sauce, mushrooms and liquid, salt, sugar and pepper. Top with shredded cheese. Cook covered over low heat 20 minutes or until noodles are tender, stirring occasionally. Sprinkle with parsley. Serve from skillet. Makes 6 servings.

Never be diverted from the truth by what you
would like to believe.

Hamburger Casserole

1 lb. hamburger
1 pkg. Tastee Taters
onion (diced)

1 can cream of mushroom or
    cream of chicken soup

Brown hamburger with onions, season to taste. Drain. Add frozen Tastee Taters and can of soup over top. Bake 400° for 30 minutes.

Hamburger Stroganoff

1/2 c. minced onion
1 clove garlic (minced)
1/4 c. butter
1 lb. ground beef
2 T. flour
1 t. salt
1/4 t. pepper

1 lb. fresh mushrooms (sliced)
    or 1 8-oz. can mushrooms, drained
1 can cream of chicken soup
    (undiluted)
1 c. commercial sour cream
parsley

Saute onion and garlic in butter over medium heat. Stir in meat and brown. Stir in flour, salt, pepper, and mushrooms. Cook 5 minutes. Stir in soup. Simmer uncovered 10 minutes. Stir in sour cream. Heat through. Garnish with parsley. Serve with noodles or rice. Makes 4-6 servings.

Wild Rice Casserole

1/2 lb. bacon (diced)
1 c. celery (diced)
1 medium onion (diced)
1/2 green pepper (diced)
1 c. wild rice

1 can cream of mushroom soup
1 can mushrooms
pimiento (optional)
Accent and seasoned salt

Wash wild rice well and place in boiling salted water. Boil about 20 minutes or until partially done; drain. Fry diced bacon, pouring off grease as necessary. Leave enough grease to saute onions, celery and green pepper, added when bacon is nearly done. Add drained wild rice along with remaining ingredients and mix well. Place in casserole, adding water to cover. Bake at 350° for 1 hour.

Jellied Pork Loaf *(Head Cheese)*

6 pork hocks
1 veal shank
10 bay leaves
1 T. whole allspice
1 T. salt

1 t. pepper
5 lb. veal shoulder (cut into
    5 or 6 pieces)
5 or 6 lb. pork butt (cut into
    5 or 6 pieces)

Combine all ingredients in 10 qt. kettle. Cover with water. Bring to a boil over high heat, reduce heat, continue cooking over medium heat for approximately 1 hour or until meat is nearly done. Remove from heat and remove meat from liquid. When cool enough to handle, cut into 1 inch cubes. Remove bay leaves and allspice from liquid. Place cubed meat back into liquid. Bring to a boil again. Cook for 45 minutes. Add seasonings to taste. Ladle into loaf pans, allowing liquid to cover meat. Cool. Then refrigerate. Makes two 4 lb. loaves.

Scalloped Tuna and Potatoes

5 cooked potatoes
1 7-oz. can tuna
1 T. onion (diced)

1 can condensed celery soup
paprika

Slice potatoes and flake tuna. Fill greased casserole with alternate layers of potatoes, tuna, onion and celery soup until all used. Pour oil from tuna over mixture and sprinkle with paprika. Bake in hot oven, 425°, about 30 minutes.

Salmon Scallop

1 can (1 lb.) salmon
6 large potatoes
1 onion (sliced thin)
1 t. salt
2 T. butter

2 c. milk
1 egg
1/4 c. fine dry bread crumbs
salt

In a buttered 2 qt. casserole, arrange layers of potatoes, fish, onion and salt, beginning and ending with a layer of potatoes. Dot with butter. Mix the egg and milk together and pour over the potato mixture. Sprinkle bread crumbs on top. Bake in a 375° oven for 1 hour or until potatoes are done.

Tuna Noodle Dish

1/2 lb. noodles
1 can mushroom soup
1/2 c. milk

1 can tuna
1/2 c. peas
potato chips

Boil noodles and drain well. Pour into casserole dish. Add mushroom soup and milk. Flake tuna; add with peas. Top with crushed potato chips. Bake at 350° for half an hour.

Tuna and Chips Casserole

1 can mushroom soup
1/2 c. milk
potato chips

1 can (7 oz.) tuna
1 c. cooked peas

Empty soup into 1 qt. casserole, mix in milk. Crush potato chips between sheets of wax paper, repeat until you have 1-1/4 cups. Drain oil or water from tuna. Add tuna to soup in casserole, then add 1 c. crushed chips, and peas. Sprinkle top with 1/4 c. chips, bake at 350° for 25 to 30 minutes. 3-4 servings.

Chopped Beef Delux

1 T. butter
1 medium onion (chopped)
1 lb. hamburger

1 can green beans (drained)
1 can tomato soup
2 c. mashed potatoes

Brown onion in butter. Add hamburger and simmer 10 minutes. Drain. Put meat, onion, green beans and soup in a 2 qt. casserole. Cover with mashed potatoes. Bake at 375° for 35 minutes.

Spaghetti Sauce

1-1/2 c. onion (chopped)
1-1/2 lbs. ground beef
1 small minced clove of garlic
1/2 to 1 T. chili powder
1 T. Worcestershire sauce
1/2 t. dried basil

1/2 c. green pepper (diced)
1/2 t. salt
1/2 c. mushrooms
2 cans tomato paste (10 oz.)
1 No. 2 can tomatoes

Cook 15 lb. pressure for 20 minutes. Serve over spaghetti. 8 servings.

Preacher's Casserole

3/4 lb. ground beef
1/4 lb. ground pork
4 medium onions (chopped)
2 c. celery (finely chopped)
2 c. chow mein noodles
   (save 1/4 c. for topping)

1 can cream of mushroom soup
1 can tomato soup
1-1/4 c. water
1 t. chili powder
salt and pepper to taste

Brown meat, add onions and celery and cook until vegetables are clear. Mix in remaining ingredients. Pour into greased casserole, top with 1/4 c. noodles (crushed), and bake in 350° oven for 45 minutes.

Holiday Lutefisk

2 lb. lutefisk
1 qt. water
2 T. salt

butter (melted)
allspice
White Sauce

Cut the fish into large pieces and tie in a cheesecloth. Bring water to a boil in large pot. (Do not use aluminum.) Add salt. Lower the fish into the water and cook about 10 minutes (simmer). Remove fish to serving dish. Serve with the butter, white sauce; sprinkle with allspice.

BASIC WHITE SAUCE

2 T. butter
2 T. flour

1 c. milk
salt

Melt butter in saucepan and stir in flour until smooth. Slowly stir in the milk and cook, stirring constantly until smooth and thick. Salt to taste.

Soups and Vegetables

Vegetable Soup—Pressure Saucepan

1 lb. soup meat
1 small soup bone
4 c. water
2 t. salt
1/4 c. unwashed rice or barley
1/2 c. onions (chopped, if desired)

2 c. tomatoes
1/4 c. potatoes (diced)
1/3 c. carrots (diced)
1/4 c. green beans (chopped)
1/4 c. celery (diced)
1 t. parsley (minced)

Cook soup meat, bone, water and salt for 17 minutes at 15 lb. pressure. Cool. Add remaining ingredients. Cook 3 minutes at 15 lb. pressure.

Cabbage and Barley Soup

1 small cabbage
1/2 c. barley
1 medium carrot
2 c. water

1/2 small onion (diced)
1 c. (cut up) left-over beef roast
1 T. salt
Dash of pepper

Cook barley until almost soft, add the water, cabbage, carrot, onion, salt and meat. Simmer until cabbage is tender, more water can be added if a thinner soup is desired.

Tomato Soup

1/4 c. rice
1/2 small onion (diced)
1 c. leftover roast

1 can whole tomatoes
1 T. salt
dash of pepper

Cook rice until tender in about 1 cup of water, add the tomatoes, roast, onion, seasonings. Simmer about 1 hour.

Old Fashioned Split Pea Soup

1 c. split peas
1 hambone or pieces of cubed ham
1 carrot (grated)
2 medium onions (minced)
1 potato (grated)

1/4 c. celery (diced)
1/4 c. green pepper (finely chopped)
salt and pepper to taste
6 c. boiling water

Cover peas with boiling water. Let soak for 1 hour. Add hambone, carrot, onions, potato, celery and green pepper. Season with salt and pepper. Simmer until peas are tender. Add water, if needed. Simmer for 5 to 10 minutes longer. Yield: 4 servings.

Bean Soup

2 c. dried white beans
8 c. boiling water
2-3 ham hocks or a ham bone
1 pkg. dry onion soup mix
1/2 c. catsup

1 t. salt
1/2 t. savory (optional)
3 stalks celery (chopped)
1 large carrot (diced fine)
pepper (to taste)

Wash and sort beans, place in large kettle. Cover with boiling water. Simmer until beans are plump. Add ham bone or hocks, soup mix, carrot, catsup, savory, salt and pepper. Cook until beans are almost tender. Add celery and more water, up to 5 cups. Simmer until celery is tender.

Chili

2 T. fat or oil
1 lb. ground beef
1/2 lb. ground lean pork
1-1/2 c. onion (chopped)
1 c. celery (diced)
1 small clove garlic (chopped fine)
1/2 green pepper (diced)

2 c. canned tomatoes
1 to 2 T. chili powder
2 T. cold water
2 t. salt
1 t. sugar
1 t. Worcestershire sauce
4 c. canned kidney beans

Melt fat, add meat, fry until lightly browned. Add onions, celery, green pepper, garlic; continue frying and stirring until onions are golden brown, about 10 minutes. Add tomatoes, chili powder, water, sugar, salt, and Worcestershire sauce. Bring to boil and then reduce to simmer for 1 hour, covered. Drain beans and add. Cook to desired thickness, uncovered (add more water if necessary). Serves 6.

Hamburger Soup

2 T. fat
1-1/2 lbs. ground beef
1-1/2 qts. water
2 c. potatoes (diced)
1 c. celery (diced)
3 t. salt

1 c. carrot (diced)
1/2 c. onion
2 c. tomatoes
1 c. rutabaga (diced)
1/4 c. rice

Brown meat. Add vegetables, seasonings and water. Bring to a boil and simmer for 1 hour.

Corn Chowder

1 c. potatoes (diced)
1 c. boiling water
3 slices bacon (cut in small pieces)
1 medium onion (chopped)

1-1/2 c. canned whole kernel corn
1 c. milk
salt and pepper to taste
2 T. parsley (chopped; optional)

Cook potatoes in water in covered pan for 10-15 minutes. Fry bacon until some of the fat is cooked out. Add onion and cook until onion is soft and bacon is browned. Add bacon, onion and corn to potatoes; cook slowly (simmer) until potatoes are done; add milk, salt and pepper. Heat just to boiling. Sprinkle with parsley after pouring into 4 serving bowls.

Hamburger Soup

3/4 lb. ground beef
1/2 c. onion (chopped)
1 can tomatoes (20 oz.)
2 c. potatoes (diced)
1 c. carrots (diced)

1/2 c. celery
1/4 c. rice (uncooked)
1-1/2 qts. water
2 t. salt

Brown the ground beef and onion. Add all other ingredients. Simmer 1 hour or more.

People seldom want to walk over
you until you lie down.

Green Bean Casserole

1 16-oz. can green beans
1 c. French fried onions

1 can cream of mushroom soup
1/2 c. sharp cheddar cheese

Drain beans, reserve 1/4 c. liquid. Alternate layers of beans and onions in baking dish. Mix liquid with mushroom soup and pour over vegetables. Sprinkle grated cheese over top and bake in 350° oven about 30 minutes.

Ground Beef Soup

1 medium onion (diced)
3 T. cooking oil
1 lb. ground beef
1 t. salt
1/2 t. pepper
Celery salt to taste
Onion salt to taste
Garlic salt to taste
2 T. parsley flakes

2 T. Worcestershire sauce
1/2 c. rice
2 potatoes (diced)
3 carrots (diced)
2 stalks celery (chopped)
1 - No. 303 can tomatoes
1 c. cooked elbow macaroni
1 can tomato sauce

Saute onion in oil in a large kettle. Add beef, seasonings, parsley flakes and Worcestershire sauce. Stir over medium heat until beef is browned. Add rice, potatoes, carrots, celery, and about 2 qts. of water. Bring to a boil. Stir well; reduce heat.

Simmer until rice and vegetables are tender. Add tomatoes, macaroni, and tomato sauce; mix well. Add water if necessary. Return to boil. Reduce heat; simmer until heated through. Yield: 8 servings.

Carrot Ring

2 T. butter
2 T. flour
1/8 t. black pepper
2 eggs

1/2 c. milk
salt to taste
dash of ginger
2 c. mashed carrots

Make white sauce by melting butter. Blend in flour and add milk and cook until thickened, stirring constantly. Remove from heat and add seasonings, beaten egg yolks and carrots. Fold in stiffly beaten whites and pour into buttered ring or bowl. Set in pan of water to bake in moderate oven, 325°, until firm.

Corn Chowder

5 medium size potatoes	1 can cream style corn
1/4 lb. salt pork (cubed)	1 c. milk
1 medium size onion	Salt and pepper

Cube potatoes, cook until done in boiling water. While potatoes are cooking, fry salt pork with onion until slightly brown. Add to drained potatoes. Add corn and milk. Season with salt and pepper to taste and reheat.

"School" Baked Beans

3 lb. beans	1/2 lb. cubed bacon
1-1/2 c. brown sugar	1 T. salt
1-1/2 c. catsup	dash of pepper
1 small onion (cut up)	water to almost cover beans

Soak beans overnight; then drain. Put beans and all ingredients in pressure cooker and cook for 55 minutes at 15 lb. pressure.

Pressure Cooker Baked Beans

1 lb. navy beans	4 heaping T. brown sugar
1/2 lb. salt pork	6 T. catsup
3 slices bacon	1 large onion

Soak beans overnight. In morning drain off water. Cut up pork and bacon and onions. Put all in pressure cooker. Add enough water to just cover beans. Stir enough to blend all ingredients well. Cook for 40 minutes at 15 lb. pressure.

Rutabaga Loaf

1 medium rutabaga	2 T. brown sugar
2 T. flour	1 egg
1/2 c. milk	2 T. butter
Nutmeg (optional)	

Cook rutabaga in salted water until soft. Mash and add butter, flour, milk, and other ingredients. Pour into greased pan. Sprinkle with fine bread crumbs. Dot with butter. Sprinkle nutmeg, if desired and bake 350° until top is brown.

Meatball and Lentil Soup

1 lb. lentils (rinse, drain)	1 1-lb. can stewed tomatoes
2 t. salt	1/2 t. marjoram
1 bay leaf	1/2 t. salt
2-1/2 qts. water	1/8 t. pepper
Meatballs (recipe follows)	1 c. sliced carrots (1/2 inch thick)
1 c. onions (chopped)	1 c. sliced celery (1/2 inch thick)
1/3 c. bacon drippings or margarine	

Combine lentils, salt, bay leaf, and water in a large (6 qt.) kettle. Bring to a boil. Reduce heat and simmer, covered for 45 minutes. Do not drain. Prepare meatballs.

Saute onion in bacon drippings. Stir in tomatoes, marjoram, salt, and pepper. Bring to a boil. Combine with cooked lentils, meatballs, carrots and celery. Bring to a boil. Cover. Simmer for 30 minutes. Makes 3-1/2 qts.

MEATBALLS

1 lb. ground beef	2 T. parsley (finely chopped)
1 c. dry bread crumbs	1 garlic clove (minced)
2 eggs (beaten)	3/4 t. salt
1/4 c. milk	1/2 t. marjoram
2 T. onion (chopped)	1/8 t. pepper

Mix lightly and shape into 15 meatballs. Brown in 1/4 c. hot oil. Drain and set aside.

Easy Onion Rings

1 large sweet onion	2 eggs (beaten)
1-1/2 c. corn meal mix or self rising corn meal	2/3 c. milk

Cut onion horizontally into slices about 1/4 inch thick. Separate to form rings. Let stand in cold water about 15 minutes. Combine 1 c. corn meal mix, eggs, and milk and stir well. Drain onion rings. Coat with 1/2 c. dry corn meal mix, dip into batter. Fry in hot deep fat, 375°, until golden brown turning once. Drain on absorbent paper. Sprinkle with salt. Serve hot.

French Fried Onion Rings

bowl of milk   water
pancake mix   sweet onions

Soak onion rings in milk for about an hour. Dip soaked rings into dry pancake mix, then into batter mix. (Batter mix is made by using equal parts of pancake mix and water.) Deep fry at 400° until golden brown (2-3 minutes). Drain. Try this recipe also for chicken, shrimp, scallops and chops. Delicious and different.

Rutabaga Hot Dish

Boil until soft:
2 rutabagas   salt
2 or 3 medium potatoes

Mash; add a little cream or milk, salt and sugar to taste, also butter. Place in casserole. Dot with butter and sprinkle with ground allspice. Heat through in 350° oven for 20-30 minutes.

Rutabaga Casserole

3 lb. rutabaga (cook, mash)   1/2 c. oleo
1/2 c. milk   2 T. cream of wheat
1/2 t. salt   1/2 c. dark Karo syrup
Dash of pepper

Combine ingredients. Bake 1 hour at 350°.

Sweet and Sour Cucumbers

4 jumbo cucumbers   2 c. white vinegar
2 T. salt   1/2 t. pepper
1 c. sugar

Sprinkle salt over thinly sliced cukes. Let stand 1 hour. Drain and squeeze out liquid. Boil remaining ingredients. Let cool. Pour over cucumbers and let marinate for several hours.

Deviled Corn

2 cans whole kernel corn (drained)
Liquid from corn
2 T. flour

colby or mild cheese
Ritz cracker crumbs
butter or oleo

Drain corn, saving liquid. Put corn into casserole dish. Mix liquid with flour until smooth. Pour over corn. Grate enough cheese to make a 1/2 inch layer over corn. Roll Ritz crackers into crumbs and mix with melted butter or oleo. Sprinkle over cheese. Bake in hot oven 1/2 hour or until crumbs are brown.

Mustard Beans

1-1/2 c. sugar
3/4 c. cider vinegar
1/4 c. prepared mustard
1/4 t. salt

1/4 t. celery seed
1/4 t. turmeric
2 cans wax beans, drained

Combine all ingredients except beans in saucepan. Bring to a boil, add beans. Simmer 5 minutes. Pack into sterilized jars and seal. Makes one pint. Delicious served cold with baked ham.

Budget: A mathematical confirmation of your suspicions.

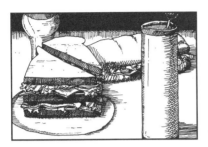

Sandwiches, Appetizers and Beverages

Ham Bunwiches

1/2 lb. boiled or baked ham
1/2 lb. sharp process cheese
1 2-3/4 oz. bottle green olives, drained

1 small onion
1/2 c. catsup
12 hamburger buns

Put ham, cheese, olives and onion through grinder. Stir in catsup. Spread between buns. Wrap each in foil, refrigerate until serving time. Heat in slow oven, 300°, until cheese melts, about 20 minutes.

Bar B Q Wieners

1 onion
2 T. vinegar
1 T. flour
1 t. paprika

1 t. chili powder
1/2 c. catsup
2 t. brown sugar
2 t. hot water

Mix all ingredients, pour over wieners in covered baking dish and bake for 1 hour.

Good Sandwiches

2 slices dark rye bread
1 slice Swiss cheese
corned beef

2 T. sour cream
2 T. sauerkraut

Heat sauerkraut and cream. Place on corned beef and cheese. Cut and serve while warm.

Turkey Joes

2 T. oleo
1/4 c. onion (chopped)
1/4 c. water
1 t. mustard
1/2 c. catsup

2 c. turkey (chopped, cooked)
1 c. chicken gumbo soup
1 t. Worcestershire sauce
salt
6 hamburger buns

In a skillet combine oleo and onion. Cook until onion is tender. Stir in remaining ingredients. Simmer for 30 minutes. Serve on hamburger buns.

Open-Face Hamburger

1 lb. ground beef
1/4 c. onion (chopped)
2 T. green pepper

3 T. catsup
Salt and pepper

Spread above ingredients, mixed, on bun halves, dot with butter and broil 7 to 10 minutes.

Reuben Sandwiches

18 slices rye bread
1-1/4 c. Thousand Island dressing
12 slices cheese

1/2 c. sauerkraut
24 slices corned beef
oleo

Spread bread with dressing. On each of 12 slices bread, arrange 1 slice cheese, 2 t. sauerkraut and 2 slices corned beef. Stack these bread slices to make 6 sandwiches. Cover with remaining bread slices. Secure with picks. Spread outside surfaces with oleo and grill until cheese is melted. Cut diagonally into 3 pieces.

Coney Islands

1/2 lb. cheese (cut in
   small cubes)
1 can Spam or Treet
1/2 c. chili sauce

2 hard boiled eggs (chopped fine)
1/3 c. onion
1/2 c. sliced pimiento olives
3 T. salad dressing

Mix all together. Fill hamburger buns. Wrap in tin foil. Heat 15-20 minutes in 350° oven. Serve hot.

Spam on a Bun

1/4 lb. processed cheese   mayonnaise
1 can Spam

Grind together cheese and Spam. Add mayonnaise until mixture is spreadable. Spread on buttered buns. Wrap in foil. If individually wrapped, bake 15 minutes at 350°.

Gooey Buns

1 lb. large bologna   1/3 c. mayonnaise
3/4 lb. American cheese   1 T. onion (minced)
1/4 c. prepared mustard   2 T. sweet pickle (chopped)

Grind bologna and cheese, add remaining ingredients and mix well. Cut hot dog buns open, spread with butter, then filling; wrap each bun in foil. Heat in slow oven, 325°, for 25 minutes. Makes 12. Great for teenagers.

Hamburger Goo

1 lb. ground beef   1/2 t. dry mustard
1 c. celery (diced)   3/4 c. catsup
1/2 c. onion (diced)   2 T. flour
1 T. brown sugar   6 hamburger buns
2 T. vinegar

Brown meat, celery and onion. Add 1 T. fat if meat is lean. Add all other ingredients, simmer about 20 minutes. Serve in toasted, buttered buns. Serves 6.

Sloppy Joes

2 lb. hamburger   2 T. Worcestershire sauce
1 c. catsup   1/3 c. mustard
2 T. brown sugar   1/2 c. water
2 onions   salt and pepper
2 T. vinegar   garlic salt

Brown hamburger in fry pan and add rest of the ingredients, stirring as you go along. Simmer for 2 hours.

Mom's Barbecue

1 lb. ground beef
2 T. fat
1 c. onions (chopped)
2 c. celery (chopped, optional)
1 green pepper (chopped, optional)
1 T. sugar

2 T. prepared mustard
1 T. vinegar
2 c. catsup
1/8 t. ground cloves
Salt to taste

Brown meat and onions in fat. Add remaining ingredients. Stir often. Simmer 30 minutes or until all vegetables are cooked. Note: 1 can tomato sauce may be substituted for part of catsup for a less spicy barbecue.

Baked Tuna Buns

1/2 lb. mild cheese
4 hard cooked eggs
2 cans chunk style tuna (2 c.)
1/2 c. hot dog relish

butter or margarine
12 hamburger buns
24 stuffed olives (optional)

Early in the day, in a large bowl, grate cheese on medium grater. Place eggs on top of grated cheese and chop (a pastry blender does a quick job.) Add tuna, relish, mayonnaise, toss to blend. Butter split buns, fill with tuna mixture. Make a 1 inch wide well in center top of each and set 2 olives in it. Wrap in foil, refrigerate. About 30 minutes before serving, start heating oven to 450°. Bake rolls 15 minutes. Makes 12.

Cheese Spudniks

Potatoes (mashed)
1 T. parsley (chopped or dry)
corn flake or cracker crumbs

cheese
1/2 c. butter or margarine

Excellent use of leftover mashed potatoes or instant mashed potatoes can be mixed according to directions and used. Add parsley to potatoes. Cut cheese into approximately 1/2 inch squares. Form potato around cheese square, roll in melted butter and then in crumbs. Place in shallow pan or dish and bake in 400° oven for 10 to 20 minutes until browned. Can be made early and chilled before baking.

Hot Spiced Tea

1 small jar Tang
1 c. sugar
1 pkg. lemonade mix

2/3 c. powdered instant tea
1 t. cinnamon
1 t. cloves

Mix all ingredients together and store in a covered jar. Use 2 or 3 t. to 1 c. boiling water.

Friendship Tea

1 7-oz. jar Tang
1/3 c. Lipton Instant tea
3/4 c. sugar

1/2 pkg. Wyler's dry lemonade
1/2 t. cloves
1/2 t. cinnamon

Mix and store in container on shelf. Use 2 t. per cup of boiling water.

Ice Cream Punch

10 c. chilled pineapple juice
1-1/2 pt. orange sherbet

3-1/2 c. vanilla ice cream
1 qt. ginger ale

Combine juice, sherbet, and ice cream in bowl. Using electric mixer or hand beater, blend well. Gently stir in ginger ale. Serve immediately. Makes about 36 punch cups.

Wedding Reception Punch

6 pkg. Kool-Aid
4 c. sugar
8 qts. water
2 46-oz. can Hawaiian Punch

1 46-oz. can pineapple juice
2 large cans frozen orange juice
1 small can frozen lemonade
1 large bottle 7-Up

Mix all ingredients. Chill before serving. Serves 50-60.

Orange Punch

5 large cans orange drink (Hi C)
1 large can apricot nectar
4 (24 oz.) bottles ginger ale
1 large can pineapple-grapefruit drink

1 lemon ice ring made with 1 pkg.
    lemonade or orange Kool-Aid
    frozen in ring mold

Hot Chocolate

10 qts. Carnation instant dry milk
   (10 envelopes)
1 lb. Nestle's Quik

1 lb. powdered sugar
6 oz. Coffee Mate

Mix all ingredients and store dry (covered) on shelf. Use 1/3 c. of mix with 1 c. boiling water. (Very nice for college students).

Hot Spiced Mocha

6 c. milk
1/2 c. instant cocoa mix

1/4 c. instant coffee
Sugar and cinnamon

Heat milk to scalding in saucepan; stir in cocoa mix and coffee. Beat until foamy. Pour into serving cups; sprinkle with cinnamon-sugar. Makes 6 cups.

Red Devil Punch

3 large cans apple juice
   or apple cider
1/2 c. red cinnamon candies

2 sticks cinnamon
1 whole orange
15 whole cloves

Heat apple juice, add red hots (cinnamon) candies and cinnamon sticks; simmer about 15 minutes. Add orange studded with cloves, simmer 10-15 minutes longer. Pour into heat proof punch bowl, float orange for decoration. Serve hot.

7-Up Red Satin Punch

1 qt. apple juice
2 pts. cranberry juice

10 (7 oz.) bottles 7-Up
Ice cubes

Chill juices and pop. At serving time combine all ingredients, adding 7-Up last. Makes about 35 punch cups.

7-Up Evergreen Bowl

4 pts. lime sherbet

12 (7-oz.) bottles 7-Up

Spoon 3 pts. of sherbet into punch bowl. Let soften at room temperature 5-10 minutes. Slowly pour in chilled 7-Up, stirring slightly. Float scoops of remaining sherbet on top. About 36 servings.

Cream Cheese Dip

1 3-oz. pkg. cream cheese
2 t. cream
2 T. catsup

2 t. French dressing (oily type)
1 t. onion (grated)
Dash of salt

Combine all ingredients well, serve with potato chips.

Cottage Cheese Dip

1-1/2 c. creamed cottage cheese
   (12 oz.)
1 T. milk or sour cream
Season as desired

1 t. finely minced onion
   (or use chives cottage cheese)
1 T. lemon juice

Use blender or mixer to thoroughly blend ingredients. Cover dish tightly and refrigerate until ready to serve. Makes about 1-1/2 cups.

Hot Beef Dip

1/4 c. onions (chopped)
1 T. oleo
1 c. milk
1 (8 oz.) pkg. cream cheese
1 c. dried beef (chopped)

1 3-oz. can sliced mushrooms
1/4 c. shredded Parmesan cheese
2 T. parsley (chopped)
rye bread

Cook onion in oleo until tender. Stir in milk and cream cheese, mixing until melted and well blended. Add remaining ingredients except bread. Serve hot over bread. It is especially good over the Trenary "limper" bread.

Beet Jelly

4 c. beet juice
5 c. sugar
1 pkg. Sure-Jell

2 pkg. Kool-Aid (unsweetened,
   raspberry, cherry or grape)

Boil beet juice and Sure-Jell for 3 minutes, add sugar and Kool-Aid and boil for 5 minutes.

Cheese-Burger Bites

1 c. flour (sifted)
1/4 c. butter
3 oz. sharp process cheese
meatballs (recipe follows)

3 oz. cream cheese
1/2 t. salt
1/2 t. paprika

Cream butter with cheese, salt, and paprika. Gradually add flour; mix thoroughly. Shape half of dough into 4-1/2 inch roll. Shape remaining dough into 9 inch roll. Wrap and chill at least 2 hours. Prepare meatballs. Cut 9 inch roll into 1/4 inch slices, place on ungreased cookie sheet. Top with meatballs. Cut remaining roll into 1/8 inch slices, place on top of meatballs. Bake for 12-15 minutes at 350°.

MEATBALLS

1/2 c. seasoned bread cubes
   (stuffing)
3 T. minced onion
2 T. water
1/2 lb. ground beef

1 egg
1/2 t. oregano
1/2 t. chili powder
2 large dill pickles (chopped)
1 bouillon cube (chopped dry)

Combine bread cubes and onion. Sprinkle with water, let stand 5 minutes. Add remaining ingredients, mix well. Shape into 36 small meatballs. Brown in skillet over low heat. 36 appetizers. Tip: appetizers may be shaped early in the day, refrigerate, then bake just before serving.

Cream Cheese Dip

1 6 oz. pkg. cream cheese
   (at room temperature)

1 envelope dry onion soup
milk

Blend milk and cheese to dip consistency. Stir in soup mix. Let set for at least 1 hour. More milk might be needed to make dip consistency.

Appetizer Ham Ball

2 (4-1/2 oz.) cans deviled ham
3 T. green olives (chopped)
1 T. prepared mustard

Tabasco sauce (if desired)
1 3-oz. cream cheese (softened)
2 t. milk

Blend deviled ham, olives and mustard. Form into ball on serving dish. Chill. Combine cream cheese and milk and frost ball with mixture. Keep chilled, remove from refrigerator shortly before serving with crackers.

Barbecue Sauce *(For Spareribs)*

1 medium onion (chopped)
1 T. brown sugar
4 T. lemon juice
2 T. water
2 T. vinegar

1 c. catsup
1 t. Worcestershire sauce
1/2 t. mustard
1/2 c. celery (chopped)
1/2 c. water

Mix in saucepan, bring to a boil. Pour over spareribs. Bake for 1 to 1-1/2 hours at 325°.

Bar-B-Q Sauce

4 t. onion (minced)
1 c. tomato puree
1 can tomato sauce
3/4 c. water
3 t. vinegar
2 t. Worcestershire sauce
1 t. salt

1 t. paprika
1 t. chili powder
1/4 t. cinnamon
1/2 t. pepper
dash of ground cloves
ginger

Combine all ingredients in order and mix.

Sauerkraut Relish

1/2 c. onion
1/2 c. carrots
1/2 c. celery
1/2 c. green pepper
1 large can sauerkraut

1/4 c. vinegar
1/4 c. water
1 c. sugar
1/4 c. oil

Dice onion, carrot, celery, and green pepper. Drain sauerkraut. Boil together vinegar, water and sugar. Cool, add oil and combine liquid with all vegetables. Chill overnight.

Pickled Beets

BRINE
1-1/2 c. sugar
1 c. vinegar

3 c. beet juice or water
2 T. salt

Cook beets until done. Cool, peel and cut into desired size pieces. Heat beets in brine until boiling and pack in hot jars; cover with brine and seal.

Dill Pickles

1 peck dill-size cucumbers   1-1/2 c. salt
  (4 to 5 inches)   4 qts. water

Make a canning brine of 8 qts. water, 1 qt. vinegar, and 2 c. salt and boil 10 minutes. Let this brine stand overnight.

In the morning drain cucumbers and place in sterilized jars with small bunches of dill. 1 t. of mustard seed may also be added to each quart with the dill. Pack cucumbers tight. Cover cucumbers in jar with the cold canning brine, being sure brine covers cucumbers. Put on cap, screwing band tight. These will ferment in 3 or 4 days.

Special Watermelon Pickle

3 lb. white portion of rind (cubed)   1 T. whole cloves
5 c. sugar   1 T. while allspice
1 c. cold water   1 T. stick cinnamon
2 c. cider vinegar   1 lemon slice

Let melon stand in salted water to cover overnight (2 T. salt to 1 qt. water). Drain; cover with fresh cold water. Cook until tender; drain; combine sugar, vinegar and 1 c. cold water. Tie spices in a bag and add to syrup. Boil 5 minutes, add melon, and cook until transparent, about 45 minutes. Pack in hot sterilized jars.

Green Tomato Pickles

5 qts. green tomatoes (thinly sliced)   4 c. white vinegar
8 medium onions (thinly sliced)   1 c. brown sugar
2 T. pickling spices   5 c. white sugar
3 c. brown sugar

Slice green tomatoes and onions, cover with a salt brine made with about 4 T. salt with enough water to cover vegetables. Soak at least 1 hour. Prepare syrup from remaining ingredients; drain tomatoes and onions in colander; rinse in cold water; drain thoroughly. Cook gently in syrup until onions are tender. Seal in sterilized jars. Makes 10 to 12 pints.

Beet and Cabbage Relish

1 qt. cooked beefs (shredded)
1 qt. cabbage (slaw)
1 t. pepper
1 t. salt

2 c. sugar
1 c. horseradish (grated)
1-1/2 c. cider vinegar and
   1/2 c. water mixed

Mix beets and cabbage, add salt, sugar, horseradish and pepper. Add vinegar. Pack in clean sterilized jars. Seal.

Bread and Butter Pickles

2 qt. cucumbers (sliced)
1 c. vinegar
1 c. sugar
1 t. turmeric
1 t. mustard seed

1 t. celery seed
1 t. curry powder
1/2 t. powder alum
1 t. salt

Combine all ingredients and cook 5 to 10 minutes and bottle.

My Favorite Room

Of all the rooms in my house, I like my kitchen best.

'Tis here I spend a lot of time, so come and be my guest.

There's coffee perking merrily, the cups are on the shelf.

And you are always welcome, so won't you help yourself?

Trying out a recipe can be a lot of fun,

And from my kitchen window, I can greet the morning sun.

When friends stop for a visit, or neighbors come to call,

They find me in my kitchen, my favorite room of all.

E.J. Callow

Candies

Easy Candy

2 pkg. butterscotch chips
1/2 c. peanut butter

5 c. corn flakes

Melt chips and peanut butter in top of double boiler. Stir in corn flakes, drop by spoon onto wax paper. Keep in refrigerator until ready to eat.

Mounds Bars

1 stick butter
1 can Eagle Brand sweetened
   condensed milk
2 lb. powdered sugar

1 14-oz. pkg. flake coconut
3/4 to a bar paraffin wax
milk chocolate

Melt butter over low heat, remove, add milk and sugar; gradually add coconut, kneading well with hands. Form bars and place on wax paper and chill. Melt wax and chocolate over hot water, dip bars into melted chocolate and place on wax paper to chill.

Chocolate Covered Cherries

1 large jar cherries
1 lb. powdered sugar
1/3 c. white syrup
1/2 c. butter

1 t. vanilla
1/2 bar paraffin wax
1/2 lb. milk chocolate

Drain cherries, mix sugar, syrup, butter and vanilla. Knead until smooth. Pinch off a small piece of mix and wrap around cherry. Place on well-buttered pan and chill several hours. Melt chocolate and wax over hot water. Dip cherries and place on buttered pan.

5 Pound Fudge

5 c. sugar
1 stick oleo
1 large can milk
3 pkg. chocolate chips (18 oz.)

1 large jar Marshmallow Creme
2 T. vanilla
nuts (if desired)

Boil sugar, oleo, and milk for 10 minutes. Remove from heat. Stir in remaining ingredients. Pour into buttered jelly roll pan.

Chocolate Cherry Balls

2/3 c. peanut butter
2 c. powdered sugar
1/2 c. or more nuts (chopped)
12 maraschino cherries (chopped)
4 T. oleo
1/2 t. salt

1 c. coconut (flaked)
1 6-oz. pkg. chocolate chips
  (melted)
3-1/2 t. parowax (melted; the
  kind used for top of jellies)

Mix peanut butter, oleo, powdered sugar, salt, nuts, coconut, and cherries together. Form into balls the size of walnuts with fingers. Chill in refrigerator for about 1 hour. Melt the wax and add the chocolate chips and stir until chips are melted. (Is best to do this in double boiler over hot water.) Dip the balls (about 4 or 5 at a time) into the melted wax and chocolate mixture. Remove them with a fork when chocolate coated. Place on wax paper to cool. Makes 30 to 36 balls.

Cat's Crunch

1-1/2 c. sugar
1/2 lb. butter
1/2 c. white corn syrup

8 c. popcorn
1 c. pecan halves
1/2 c. slivered almonds

Cook sugar, butter and syrup in 1-1/2 qt. saucepan until light caramel color, 10 to 15 minutes, stirring constantly. Pour over popcorn, pecans, and almonds in large flat pan. Break in pieces while warm. Store in covered container in refrigerator. Mixture keeps well.

*One should learn to disagree without
becoming disagreeable.*

Coconut Bon-Bons

Mix with spoon:
1/2 lb. butter or oleo
1 lb. powdered sugar
1/2 can Eagle Brand milk

1 bag coconut (12 oz.)
1/2 c. nuts (chopped fine)
1 t. vanilla

Form into bon-bon shapes, chill and dip into mixture of 1 lb. chocolate and 3/4 bar of paraffin wax.

Mashed Potato Candy

3/4 c. plain cold mashed potato
4 c. or more powdered sugar
4 c. sweetened coconut
1/2 t. salt

3 or 4 squares baking chocolate
1 T. butter
2 T. paraffin

Mix first 4 ingredients in bowl, adding enough confectioners' sugar to make firm mixture. Press into well buttered 9 x 13 inch pan, drop by teaspoon onto wax paper or shape into balls for chocolate centers. Let dry slightly. Melt chocolate, butter and paraffin, let set up. Cover confectioners' sugar mixture with chocolate or dip balls. Yield: about 2 lb.

Turtles

1/2 lb. light caramels
2 T. cream

pecans
semi-sweet chocolate chips

Melt caramels and cream over hot water. Butter baking sheet and arrange pecans on it. Spoon caramel over nuts. Let stand 30 minutes. Melt chips in double boiler and spread over all sides of turtles.

Butterscotch Sauce

1 egg yolk
1/4 c. water
1/3 c. light syrup

2/3 c. brown sugar
1/4 c. butter

Mix egg yolk, water, syrup, and sugar. Add butter and cook over low heat until slightly thickened. Beat well just before using. Serve hot or cold.

Maple Divinity

2 c. maple flavored syrup
1/4 t. salt

2 egg whites
1/2 c. broken pecans

Butter sides of heavy 2 qt. saucepan. In it, cook syrup rapidly over high heat to hard ball stage, 250°, without stirring. Remove from heat. At once add salt to egg whites, beating constantly with mixer at high speed. Continue beating until soft peaks form and it begins to lose gloss. Quickly add nuts. Drop with teaspoon on wax paper on cookie sheet, swirl each candy to a peak. Makes about 2 dozen candies.

Popcorn Balls

2 c. sugar
4 T. vinegar
1/2 c. water

2 T. butter
popcorn (popped previously)

Mix sugar, vinegar, water and butter, bring to a boil. Cook to hard ball stage, pour over popcorn. Form into balls, dipping hands in cold water while shaping.

Candied Popcorn

1/2 c. light corn syrup
1/2 c. sugar
1/2 t. salt

1 t. vanilla (optional)
food coloring (optional)
2 qts. popped corn

Mix together in heavy saucepan, corn syrup, sugar and salt and bring to a boil. Cook 2 minutes over medium heat, stirring constantly. Stir in vanilla and food coloring. Pour over popped corn in large bowl and stir until corn is evenly coated with mixture. Spread margarine on hands and press popcorn into balls or other desired shapes.

Sour Cream Candy

2 c. sugar
1/2 t. salt
1 c. sour cream

2 T. butter
1/2 to 1 c. nuts (pecans or walnuts)

Cook on medium heat to soft ball stage, 236°. Add butter. Cool to 110°. Then beat until it loses gloss. Add nuts and pour into buttered pan. Cut when cool.

Popsicles

1 envelope unflavored gelatin
Cold water
3/4 c. sugar

1-1/2 c. boiling water
1 envelope Kool-Aid (unsweetened)

Dissolve gelatin in cold water according to package directions. Combine boiling water and Kool-Aid, add gelatin. Add water to make 1 qt. of liquid. Stir in sugar. Pour into molds and freeze. Jello can be substituted for gelatin.

Date Candy

1-3/4 c. Date Butter
1/2 c. nuts (chopped)

1/2 c. flaked coconut
1/4 c. sliced candied cherries

DATE BUTTER

2 7-oz. packages pitted dates

3/4 c. water

Cut up dates and cook with water over medium heat for about 10 minutes, until dates are mushy.

Blend ingredients, chill. Shape into balls, then roll in additional coconut. Coconut and cherries add bright contrast to dates. Makes about 30 candies.

Candy Strawberries

2 (3 oz.) pkg. strawberry gelatin
1 c. ground pecans
1 c. flaked coconut
3/4 c. sweetened condensed milk

1/2 t. vanilla
red decorating sugar
blanched almonds (sliced)

Combine gelatin, pecans and coconut. Stir in milk and vanilla; mix well. Chill 1 hour. Shape into strawberries and roll in red sugar. If you wish, tint sliced almonds with green food coloring and insert in tops of berries to form leaves. Makes 1 lb. 3 oz.

Hot Fudge Sauce

1 c. granulated sugar
1/4 c. flour
1/4 t. salt
3 sq. baking chocolate

1-3/4 c. evaporated milk (1 tall can)
1 T. butter
1 t. vanilla

Combine sugar, flour and salt in a qt. size measuring pitcher or bowl; set aside. Combine chocolate and evaporated milk in top of double boiler; over very hot (not boiling) water cook and stir until chocolate is melted and blended with milk. Very gradually add hot mixture to dry ingredients, beating until smooth, between additions. Return mixture to double boiler; continue to stir and cook over boiling water until slightly thickened, about 10 minutes. Remove from heat; stir in butter and vanilla. Cool slightly before serving over ice cream. Makes 2-1/4 cups. Note: If sauce is not served immediately, cover pan to prevent formation of "skin" on surface. Leftover sauce may be refrigerated in an air tight container and rewarmed over hot water just until softened.

Mints

2-1/2 c. powdered sugar
1 3-oz. pkg. Philadelphia
  Cream Cheese

1/2 t. flavoring
drop of coloring

COLOR
pink
white
green
yellow

FLAVOR
vanilla
almond
peppermint
lemon

Knead as for pie dough to distribute coloring and flavoring. Dip in granulated sugar and mold. Let dry several hours. Keep refrigerated. Note: purchase molds in candy making shop.

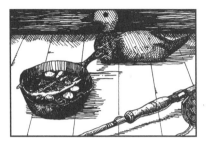

Wild Game

Fried Venison

venison from the hind quarter
  of the deer
3/4 c. flour
Dash of salt and pepper

1/4 lb. butter or margarine
1 medium onion
1 can cream of mushroom soup

Take venison and slice into thin steaks. Roll meat in a flour and pepper mixture, then drop into a skillet of melted butter and browned onion slices. Fry until meat is well done, then add 1 can of cream of mushroom soup which acts as a delicious gravy.

Fish Baked in Milk

2 T. butter
1-1/2 lb. fish
1 t. salt

2/3 c. water
2/3 c. evaporated milk

Melt butter in baking pan. Place fish in pan, sprinkle with salt, add water and milk. Bake in moderate oven, 350°, until fish is tender, about 45 minutes. Serves 6.

Baked Partridge

1 partridge
dash of paprika

salt and pepper
1 can cream of mushroom soup

Clean and wash bird thoroughly, then cut into pieces like you would a chicken. Brown pieces in skillet and season with salt, pepper and paprika. Remove from skillet and place in a casserole dish. Cover with mushroom soup and 1/2 can water. Bake 1 hour at 450°.

Partridge Pie

Cook 1 partridge in a saucepan with water to cover for about 3/4 of an hour. Let it cool, and then take the meat off the bones and cut into small pieces. Peel and cut up:

2 medium carrots   2 stalks of celery (cut up fine)
1 medium onion   1 c. rutabaga (cubed)
2 medium potatoes

Cook the vegetables in a pan with water to cover, until almost tender, add the partridge meat and cook another 10 minutes. Thicken the liquid with a flour and water mixture (2 tablespoons flour and about 3 T. water). Cover casserole with a pastry or drop biscuits and bake about 15 or 20 minutes until brown.

Barbecued Rabbit

Fry 2 or 3 rabbits until well browned. Add 1/2 cup water and simmer for 1/2 hour. Make sauce while rabbit is simmering.

SAUCE

1 can tomatoes (large)   1 small onion (chopped)
1 can tomato paste (medium)   3 cloves garlic
1 can tomato sauce (large)   2 T. brown sugar
1 small can mushrooms with liquid   1 T. vinegar

Add sauce to rabbit and simmer about an hour more, adding water during cooking if it begins to stick.

Benny's Fish Boil *(serves 20)*

2 gallons of water—bring to a boil
ADD:
1-1/2 c. iodized salt   20 medium potatoes (with skins)
Boil 15 minutes.

ADD:
15 medium onions (peeled)
Boil 10 minutes.
8 lbs. fish (whitefish, german brown lake trout or coho)

Cut in 1-1/2 inch steaks, leaving skin and bones on. Boil 10 to 12 minutes. Serve on separate dishes, with drawn butter.

Frank's Way with Northerns

Wash whole fish and pat dry with paper towel. Lay out on strip of aluminum foil. Sprinkle cavity with salt and pepper. Loosely wrap foil around fish, sealing edges well. Wrap with another strip of foil so fish is double wrapped. Put on cookie sheet and place in preheated 400° oven for 25 minutes.

Open foil. Remove skin by gently rubbing with paper towel. (Skin will be picked up easily by towel). Separate fish along the back bone with spatula and discard bone skeleton. Place on platter and drizzle with melted butter and a hint of paprika. You may also cook in the fireplace, but you must turn occasionally. There are no lingering fish cooking odors in the house with this recipe.

Rabbit and Chicken Booyah

1 or 2 large chickens (cut up)   6 medium carrots (diced)
1 or 2 rabbits (cut up)   1/2 bunch of celery (diced)
1 small rutabaga (diced)   8 medium potatoes (diced)
2 large onions (diced)   salt and pepper to taste

Cook cut up chicken and rabbit in large kettle with water to cover. Add seasoning. When meat is done, cool and remove meat from bones. Put vegetables in the kettle and cook until tender. Add cubed chicken and rabbit, heat thoroughly and serve.

Fish Mojakka *(Fish Stew)*

bacon (6 strips)   garlic salt
6 potatoes   dehydrated vegetable soup
2 medium onions   pickling spice
several fish   dry milk
salt and pepper   oleo or margarine

Crisscross 6 strips of bacon in bottom of a 6 quart pot and start them sizzling. Dice 6 pared potatoes and 2 medium onions. Cut 4 fillets (2 fish) into inch square pieces. On top of bacon add a layer of onion, a layer of potatoes and a layer of fish. Repeat process until all ingredients are used up. Seasoning each layer with salt, pepper and garlic salt. Add enough water to barely cover the top layer of fish. Sprinkle 1 package of dehydrated vegetable soup over the top. Tie 1 t. pickling spice in a bag and place in pot. Bring to a boil, then cover and simmer 30 minutes. Remove spice bag. Mix 2/3 c. dry milk with 2 c. water, add to pot with 1 stick of oleo or margarine. Stir lightly. Cover and simmer 20 minutes.

Duck a la Northwoods

6 ducks (breast them out)
Cut breasts into 1 inch squares. Roll in beaten eggs and then in Bisquick. Brown in frying pan.

ADD:

1 can mushroom soup
1 can of water
1/2 green pepper (sliced up)

2 T. Worcestershire sauce
salt and pepper

Cook at 350° for 45 minutes to 1 hour. Serve over rice or potatoes.

Baked Fish Fillets

1 lb. fish fillets
1 c. milk
1 T. salt

fine dry bread crumbs
1 T. oil or butter (melted)

Cut fillets into serving pieces. Combine milk and salt. Dip fish into milk, then into crumbs, being sure fish is completely covered with crumbs. Place in greased baking dish, sprinkle with oil and brown quickly in very hot oven, 500°, 10 to 20 minutes. Do not add water. Serve with melted butter or lemon butter.

Barbecued Venison

2 lb. venison meat
1 can tomato soup
1/2 c. vinegar
1/2 c. catsup
2 t. salt
1 t. celery seed or 1/4 c. celery, chopped small

1/2 c. water
1 t. paprika
1 t. chili powder
2 T. brown sugar
garlic to taste

Trim all fat from meat. Brown meat in small amount of shortening. Combine water, soup, catsup, vinegar and seasonings. Pour over browned meat. Cover and let simmer over low heat for 2-3 hours, until meat is very tender. Water will need to be added in small amounts during cooking. Serve over cooked egg noodles.

Index

Breads

Cakes and Frostings

Candies

Sandwiches, Appetizers and Beverages

Soups and Vegetables

Strawberries

Sweet Rolls and Doughnuts

Wild Game

Avery Color Studios, Inc. has a full line of Great Lakes oriented books, puzzles, cookbooks, shipwreck and lighthouse maps and lighthouse posters.

For a full color catalog call:
1-800-722-9925

Avery Color Studios, Inc. products are available at gift shops and bookstores throughout the Great Lakes region.